AF541752

DPH SPORTS SERIES

FOOTBALL

H. C. DUBEY

DISCOVERY PUBLISHING HOUSE
New Delhi-110002

First Published-1999
Reprinted - 2014

ISBN 978-81-7141-451-2

Published by:
DISCOVERY PUBLISHING HOUSE
4831/24, Ansari Road, Prahlad Street,
Daryaganj, New Delhi-110 002 (*INDIA*)
Phone: 3279245
Fax: 91-11-3253475

Printed at:
Infinity Imaging Systems
Delhi

Sports is the only 'Sweaty' Leisure-time activity. Sports represents a moment of joy in the midst of hard poverty-stricken and dirty everyday life. Doing sports even makes one's work go more smoothly the next day.

This series will be useful to the sports promoters, organisers, coaches and other persons related or interested in sports.

Editor

PREFACE

The need of having a sports series felt because today's situation of the world is not conducive to peace, all round there is destruction, despair, conflict and war; war if not between two nations then within the country itself. In a world where there are some 820 million people unemployed or under-employed, and where 86 million people are born every year, it is not surprising that one out of every four individuals lives in absolute poverty. The *Discovery Publishing House* by Publishing this series seeks to get positive response as—to means by which sports can promote and propagate peace and international cooperation. Sportsmen form a large identifiable cadre. We visualises a situation where a conscious efforts is made all over the world to train the sportspersons to spread the message of peace and international cooperation. Instead of peace keeping efforts through arms and army, the sportspersons may be used as soldiers of peace in a subtle manner. The effort is to make the realize the contribution of sports as a factor for sustainable development, peace keeping and international cooperation.

In developing countries, sports development cooperation is still in the need of justification and steadfast arguments. Many people ask the question "why invest in sports in developing countries for which water supply, health service and agriculture projects are much better suited? An apt reply to this question may be "for many of the people of a developing country,

CONTENTS

1 INTRODUCTION

In primitive days, some kind of football was part of man's life. Stories go about gruesome tradition, that in historic times some races used their enemies severed heads as footballs. The Romans are said to have fostered football as a part of their military training. It is generally assumed that Roman soldiers brought the game to Britain.

The game of football is one of the most popular and simple game in the world. Although the modern game of football emerged in England, in its primitive form it had undoubtedly been played for centuries. The game began in England in the 12th century but Edward II banned it in 1324. His successor Edward III in 1349, Richard II in 1389 and Henry IV in 1401, as also the Scottish rulers forbade people from playing football. The monarchs could not stop the interest of people and started taking a lenient view and football became popular, at least in the public schools. Here were no definite rules of the game, each team played with its own.

An attempt was made by Thring and Dewinton to frame a uniform set of rules but Thring could succeed in doing so only after first trying them out for years. The first football rules were framed in 1862 and were revised in 1863. The same year, the Football Association of England was formed and the new rules of this game were framed in 1864.

An international football match for the first time was played between England and Scotland. Considering the growing popularity of the game, delegates from seven nations met on May 21, 1904 to form the Federation International de Football Association FIFA). FIFA organised the World Football Championship for the first time in 1930 at MONTEVIDEO and the Olympic Champion Uraguay lifted the JULES-RIMET TROPHY named after the then President of the FIFA.

Football was introduced in India by the British. Being a simple and inexpensive game, it became popular among the masses. India took part in the Olympic games held in 1948 in England. India played in the semi-final in the 1956 Olympics. India had, in fact, already made her mark as the greatest power in Asia by wining the title at the first Asian Games held in Delhi in 1951.

THE FIELD OF PLAY

The Field of Play and appurtenances shall be as shown in the following plan:

(1) The field of play shall be rectangular, its length being not more than 130 yards nor less than 100 yards and its breadth not more than 100 yards nor less than 50 yards. (In International Matches the length shall be not more than 120 yards nor less than 110 yards and the breadth not more than 80 yards nor less than 70 yards.) The length shall in all cases exceed the breadth.

(2) The field of play shall be marked with distinctive lines, not more than 5 inches in width, not by a V-shaped rut, in accordance with the plan, the longer boundary lines being called the touch-lines and the shorter the goal-lines. A flag on a post not less than 5 feet high and having a non-pointed top, shall be placed at each corner; a similar flag-post may be placed opposite the halfway-line on each side the field of play, not less than 1 yard outside the touch-line. A halfway-line shall be marked out across the field of play. The centre of the field of play shall be indicated by a suitable mark and a circle with a 10 yards radius shall be marked round it.

(3) At each end of the field of play two lines shall be drawn at right-angles to the goal-line, 6 yards from each goal-post. These shall extend into the field of play for a distance of 6 yards and shall be joined by a line drawn parallel with the goal-line. Each of the spaces enclosed by these lines and the goal-line shall be called a goal-area.

(4) At each end of the field of play two lines shall be drawn at right-angles to the goal-line, 18 yards from each goal-post. These shall extend into the field of play for a distance of 18 yards and shall be joined by a line drawn parallel with the goal-line. Each of the space enclosed by these lines and the goal-lines shall be called a penalty-area. A suitable mark shall be made within each penalty-area, 12 yards from the mid-point of the goal-line, measured along an undrawn line at right angles thereto. These shall be the penalty-kick marks. From each penalty-kick mark an arc of circle, having a radius of 10 yards, shall be drawn outside the penalty-area.

(5) From each corner-flag post a quarter circle, having a radius of 1 yard, shall be drawn inside the field of play.

(6) The Goals shall be placed on the centre of each goal-line and shall consist of two upright posts, equidistant from the corner-flags and 8 yards apart (inside measurement), joined by a horizontal cross-bar the lower edge of which shall be 8 ft. from the ground. The width and depth of the goal-posts and the width and depth of the cross-bars shall not exceed 5 inches (12 cm). The goal-posts and the cross-bars shall have the same width.

Net may be attached to the posts, cross-bars and ground behind the goals. They should be appropriately supported and be so placed as to allow the goal keeper ample room.

THE BALL

The ball shall be spherical; the outer casing shall be of leather or other approved materials. No material shall be used in its construction which might prove dangerous to the players.

The circumstance of the ball shall not be more than 28 inches and not less than 27 inches. The weight of the ball at the start of the game shall not be more than 16 oz. nor less than 14 oz. The pressure shall be equal to 0.6.1.1 atmosphere at sea level. The ball shall not be changed during the game unless authorised by the Referee.

NUMBER OF PLAYERS

(1) A match shall be played by two teams, each

consisting of not more than eleven players, one of whom shall be the goalkeeper.

(2) Substitutes may be used in any match played under the rules of an official competition at FIFA. Confederation or National Association level, subject to the following conditions:

(a) that the authority of the international association(s) or national association(s) concerned, has been obtained,

(b) that, subject to the restriction contained in the following paragraph (c) the rules of a competition shall state how many, if any, substitutes may be used, and

(c) that a team shall not be permitted to use more than two substitutes in any match who must be chosen from not more than five players whose names shall be given to the Referee prior to the commencement of the match.

(3) Substitutes may be used in any other match, provided that two teams concerned reach agreement on a maximum number, not exceeding five, and that the terms of such agreement are intimated to the Referee, before the match. If the Referee is not informed, or if the teams fail to reach agreement, no more than two substitutes shall be permitted. In all cases the substitutes must be chosen from not more than five players whose names shall be given to the Referee prior to the commencement of the match.

(4) Any of the other players may change places with the goalkeeper, provided that the Referee is

informed before the change is made, and provided also, that the change is made during a stoppage of the game.

(5) When a goalkeeper or any other player is to be replaced by a substitute, the following conditions shall be observed:

(a) the Referee shall be informed of the proposed substitution, before it is made,

(b) he shall enter the field during a stoppage in the game, and at the half-way line.

(d) A player who has been replaced shall not take any further part in he game.

(e) A substitute shall be subject to the authority an jurisdiction of the Referee whether called upon to play or not.

(f) The substitution is completed when the substitute enters the field of play, from which moment he becomes a players and the player whom he is replacing ceases to be a player.

REFEREES

A Referee shall be appointed to officiate in each game. His authority and the exercise of the powers granted to him by the Laws of the Game commence as soon as he enters the field of play.

His power of penalizing shall extend to offences committed when play has been temporarily suspended, or when the ball is out of play. His decision on points of fact connected with the play shall be final, so far as the result of game is concerned.

He shall: enforce the Laws; refrain from penalizing in

cases where he is satisfied that, by doing so, he would be giving an advantage to the offending team; keep a record of the game; act as timekeeper and allow the full or agreed time, adding thereto all time lost through accident or other cause; have discretionary power to stop the game for any infringement of the Laws and to suspend or terminate the game whenever, by reason of the elements, interference by spectators, or other cause, he deems-such stoppage necessary. In such a case he shall submit a detailed report to the competent authority within the stipulated time, and in accordance with the provisions set up by the National Association under whose jurisdiction the match was played. Reports will be deemed to be made when received in the ordinary course of post; from the time he enters the field of play, caution and show a Yellow Card to any player guilty of misconduct or ungentlemanly behaviour. In such cases the referee shall send the name of the offender to the competent authority, within the stipulated time, and in accordance with the provisions set by the National Association under whose, jurisdiction the match was played. Reports will be deemed to be made when received in the ordinary course of post; allow no person other than the players and Linesmen to enter the field of play without his permission; stop the game if, in his opinion, a player has been seriously injured; have the player removed as soon as possible from the field of play, and immediately resume the game. If a player is slightly injured, the game shall not be stopped until the ball has ceased to be in play. A player who is able to go to the touch or goal-line for attention of any kind, shall not be treated on the field of play; send off the field of play and show a red card to any player who, in his opinion is guilty of violent conduct serious foul play, the use of foul or abusive language or who persists in misconduct after having received a caution

(i) Signal for recommencement of the game after all stoppages.

(j) Decide that the ball provided for a match meets with the requirements of Law.

LINESMEN

Two Linesmen shall be appointed, whose duty shall be to indicate:

(a) when the ball is out of play,

(b) which side entitled to a corner-kick, goal-kick or throw-in,

(c) when a substitution is desired.

They shall also assist the Referee to control the game in accordance with the Laws. In the event of undue interference or improper conduct by a Linesman, the Referee shall dispense with his services and arrange for a substitute to be appointed. (The matter shall be reported by the Referee to the competent authority.) The Linesmen should be equipped with flags by the Club on whose ground the match is played.

METHOD OF SCORING

Except as otherwise provided by these Laws, a goal is scored when the whole of the ball has passed over the goal-line, between the goal-posts and under the cross-bar, provided it has not been thrown, carried or intentionally propelled by hand or arm, by a player of the attacking side, except in the case of goalkeeper who is within his own penalty-area. The team scoring the greater number of goals during a game shall be the winner; if no goals, or equal number of goals are scored, the game shall be termed a "draw".

GOAL-KICK

When the whole of the ball passes over the goal-line excluding that portion between the goal-posts either in the air or on the ground, having last been played by one of the attacking team, it shall be kicked direct into play beyond the penalty-area from any point within the goal-area by a player of the defending team. A goalkeeper shall not receive the ball into his hands from a goal-kick in order that he may thereafter kick it into play. If the ball is not kicked beyond the penalty-area, i.e., direct into play, the kick shall be retaken. The kicker shall not play the ball a second time until it has touched or been played by another player. A goal shall not be scored direct from such a kick. Players of the team opposing that of the player taking the goal-kick shall remain outside the penalty area until the ball has been kicked out of the penalty-area.

2

FOOTBALL TECHNIQUES

The techniques in football can be divided into two groups: 1. Techniques without the ball; 2. Techniques with the ball.

TECHNIQUES WITHOUT THE BALL

During a match, a player, on an average is with the ball for about 60 to 150 seconds. This naturally depends upon the nature, function and the position of the player. However, in the rest of the rest of the time, when he is without ball, he is fully involved in the game, i.e. busy in doing something or the other. A player naturally is busy either in doing something or the other. A player naturally is busy either in supporting the action of the player with the ball or in defensive action. Such as, correcting his position by running to the new position, marking his immediate opponent in order to prevent in order to prevent him from receiving the pass if made to him, interception or even reducing the possibility for the pass to him. Or he is directly confronted with the opponent in tackling to regain the possession of the ball. All these are individual actions but without ball. Therefore, the technique involved in such actions must be fully understood and are as important as the techniques with the ball. They are as follows:

a. Running without ball; b. Jumping techniques; c. Defensive position

Running without the ball

Mostly, it is seen that a football player frequently runs distances between 5 to 30 meters. It means a ;player must be able to accelerate to his maximum speed within a few steps. In other words, the ability to accelerate as quickly as possible is the first essential characteristic of his run so that he is well in time for the subsequent actions. A football player performs running movements in the absence of forceful push off from the ground. Most often he has to accelerate either from standing or from walking or jogging situation It is advisable for a player to be constantly on the move to have a flying start and save at least one tenth of a second.

Running of a football player is quite distinct from the running of an athlete. A football player is generally not free from external influences, so it is difficult for him to keep his muscles loose. However, he should try his best to do so, but at the same time. Should be ready to counter external influences such as tackling, charging, or collision. The arms of a football player do not run close to the body but slightly away from the body which helps in maintaining balance. A football player. Except when he goes for sprinting for comparatively longer distances, tries to keep his strides relatively shorter that is under his body contrary to an athlete. The sprints of a football player cannot be compared with the harmonious movements of a middle distance runner, which are very economical and rhythmic. A football player, as far as possible, tries to eliminate unnecessary and useless movements, nut at the same time, never tries to develop the perfect running style of an athlete.

Another important characteristics of running of a player is his ability to change the direction which always does not depend on his own will, e.g., a defender is running towards a forward player ;who suddenly changes his direction, so the defender has to change his direction accordingly. There is not much difference between attacker's and defender's movement of changing the direction of run. However. Must depends on who initiates the movement and the response to it.

Practice to develop the running techniques

The following are the exercises to develop the running techniques;

1. Run-up-exercises for different distances and from different starting positions, i.e., sitting, half squat, lying, turning (hall and full) performing jump before starting for running.
2. Running in curves, i.e., zig zag in circle, around the centre circle of the field or at the arc of penalty area, i.e., first running on the straight line of the penalty area and then on the top of arc outside or the penalty spot; then again turning towards the straight line of penalty area. Exercises can also be arranged by fixing the flag posts in a straight line or in a particular manner and then running around them or the players stand in one line and one of them performs zig zag running and so on.
3. Running, stopping and changing the direction according to the visual signal. Concentration on the

visual signal and quick reaction should be emphasised here;

4. Medicine balls or footballs are arranged in a line to enable the players to run over them. Distance between the two balls is such that the players are forced to take a short step, so that the frequency of the steps remains high.
5. In a small area players are hunting for each other with high intensity. A player in the front, runs freely to his will and keeps on changing his direction; the other player tries to catch him.

In all these exercises, emphasis should be laid on the fact that the players run, stop and move abruptly and then unexpectedly start sprinting. To be able to stop suddenly, the centre of gravity is shifted backward. This is achieved by lifting the trunk slightly upward from bent position while running so that the weight is shifted to the rear leg which automatically is followed by a comparatively longer stride by the other leg and the heel of the front leg will touch the ground first, thus it strikes against the ground and stops. This action is simultaneously supported by lowering the centre of gravity by bending both the legs at knee joint. In order to save valuable time, the players need to master these techniques at every stage of training.

Jumping technique

Depending on different positions of the players on the field, a football player on an average needs to jump eight to ten times in match. It has been already discussed that, the running of a player may not necessarily be for the possession of the ball immediately (positioning). But jumping action definitely is combined with heading action for various purposes. There is always a challenge for the ball in the air. But the momentary touch with the ball is decisive action. No doubt much of the things depend on the ability of the player to judge the speed and flight of the ball, the importance of timely take off and the development of the muscular force in the legs and the necessary coordination cannot be under-rated. In various games, played at different levels, it is observed that about fifty per cent of the jumps are performed after a short approach run of three steps of approach run and rest of the jumps are performed from standing position. Nintyfive per cent of the jumps, if performed after approach run are executed by having single leg take off, whereas, if it is a standing jump then the double leg take off is used for about seventy per cent of the jumps.

It necessary to mention here that it may be any type of jump, but always the jumping action is performed under the influence of the challenging opponent. That is why in training, it is not advisable to teach the techniques of athletic-jump, because the raising of the knee and the swinging leg will usually result in an infringement of the laws of the game. In most of the cases the approach run and the swinging of leg is restricted. Therefore, in training the development of elasticity, which depends on the strength and speed, should dominate, so that a player is able to jump and reach the optimum height, even when there is no time available to prepare for the jump.

Developing Jumping Techniques

1. High jumps and long jumps from standing position.

   a. Double leg take off;

   b. Single leg take off;

2. High jumps with heading technique without ball;

   a. After short approach run with single leg take off;

   b. Without approach run with double leg take off;

3. As in Exercise-2 but with ball

   a. Ball is hanged

   b. Ball is served

4. As in Exercise 3

   a. With passive opponent

   b. Active opponent

5. Situations created in penalty area, for example, from a cross pass or a corner kick, both the defenders and attacker are jumping and heading for their purposes.

Defensive position

Defensive position includes two things, first, the feints without ball by the defenders, such as feints with the upper part of the body, with legs and so on. The second aspect is the positioning by the goalkeeper just before the shot at the goal by the attacker. For example, at the time of penalty kick, a goalkeeper assumes the position in such a way that his legs are slightly opened, body weight is shifted to the toes, legs are slightly bent at the knee joints and the upper part of the body is bent forward. All these presumed positions favour fast execution of defensive action.

Techniques with the ball

The techniques with the ball are sub-divided into the following eight elements:

a. All types of kicking; b. Ball reception (with different body parts); c. Heading; d. Feinting with ball; e. Tackling; f. Dribbling; g. Throw-in; h. Techniques of goalkeeping

In the game of football, different types of kicks are applied in different ways and for different purposes. For example, kicking for passing. Passing can further be divided into passing for short distances and passing for long distances that is, it may be on the ground or in the air Kicks are also used for shooting at the goal for which a player is required to kick the ball with different parts of the foot. Kicks are also used for clearance by the defenders which definitely have altogether a different purpose. Some kicks known as specialised kicks, are taken after the infringement of the laws of the game that is free kicks. For such type of kicks, the peculiarities of the players play a significant role.

Keeping in view the purpose of the kicks, the techniques of kicking, for the sake of study, can further be classified into common kicks and uncommon kicks. Corresponding to the frequency of their application in the game, the inside of the foot kick, instep kick, inner instep kick and the outer instep kick are the most common types of kicks, whereas the outside of the foot kick, the heel kick, kicking with toes are considered less common types of kicks.

fundamentals of kicking

It is clear that the different kicks are taken for different purposes and there is no single kick which can always be taken under similar circumstances. However, irrespective of the type of kick, the influence of standing leg, the role of the foot which comes in contact with the ball and the trunk that is upper part of the body need to be made clear.

The standing leg

The standing leg with a slight difference in different types of Kicks, remains slightly bent at the knee joint, so that it bears the weight of the body during kick and also supports the transfer of force to the ball. At the time of a kick, the foot of the standing leg is kept near the ball that favours the low, short and accurate pass, but if it is kept away and behind the ball, then there is a possibility of high and long pass.

The playing leg

The demand on the playing leg at the time of kick is the fixation of foot joint, which favours the transfer of force to the ball, and the kick can be performed accurately and without any chance of injury. The initial swing of the playing leg, which is in the opposite direction of the kick, influences the impact on the ball. The playing leg naturally follows the direction of kick which is the most important fundamental which ensures accuracy, but a player should not fall on to the kicking leg immediately after the kick. This is most important for the beginners. In order to kick the ball low, the knee of the kicking leg is kept low over the ball, but for a higher trajectory in passing, the knee of the kicking leg is kept slightly behind the ball be keeping the standing leg slightly behind the ball.

The trunk action

Kick is a 'whole body movement'. For that the force is gathered and transferred from the trunk to the leg and then to the ball. To increase the force in the kick, the trunk first assumes a position so that a little arc of the back an he seen which results from the initial swing of the kicking leg and by raising the trunk slightly behind. At the same time, the arm and shoulder of the opposite side of the kicking leg is taken back. This is the actual phase when muscle force is prepared which later is transferred by lowering the trunk which should be supported by the slight bend at the knee joint of the standing leg and also by the slight bend of the body at hip joint. Shoulder opposite to the kicking leg which was taken back at the time of preparatory movement, twists forward and the arm of the respective shoulder side, swings forward to the side of kicking leg simultaneously with the completion of the kicking action.

3

OPTION FUNDAMENTALS

LINE PLAY

Offensive linemen should love triple option football. Their blocks will be the same as those used in no-option football, but blocking angles are improved and as a result the linemen will not have to make as many of the demanding, strength-against-strength blocks to make the offense work. Physical strength is necessary, of course, whether in triple option blocking or any other kind. In the triple option, however, the fact that certain defensive players are being optioned rather than blocked frees certain offensive linemen for double-team blocks or good angle blocks on other personnel.

In Figure 1, for example, with the center and guard double—teaming the noseman and the quarterback reading the defensive tackle, the offensive tackle is freed to release down on the linebacker, who must hold his position in order to play the dive back. The offensive tackle's angle block on the linebacker is far more efficient, and has a higher degree of success, than if he were required to execute a drive block on the defensive tackle.

The improved angles and easier types of blocks arise when a team is running the triple option play itself. When a conventional, non-option type of play is run, it doesn't matter what offensive alignment a team lines up in, the players still must execute its conventional blocks. The act of lining up in an option formation does not change any of the blocking assignments unless the option play is run.

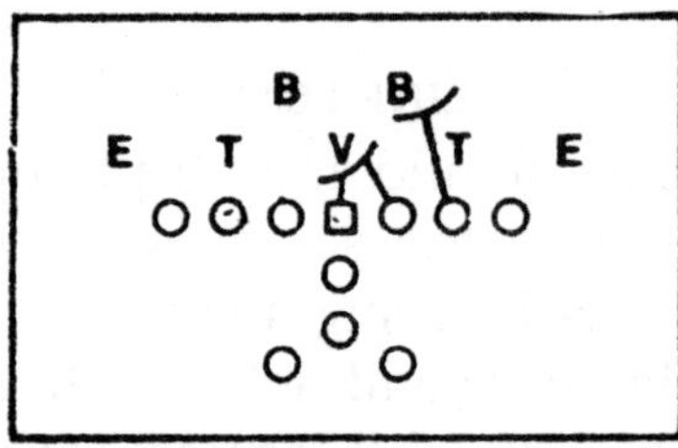

FIG. 1: Double—teaming and angle blocking

Linemen must learn to recognize the various defensive alignments and formations through constant practice before they can be expected to execute their blocking assignments effectively. Defensive alignment affects the blocking of the entire offensive line, and in many cases changes the personnel the players are responsible for blocking.

Coaches sometimes spend so much time working with the offensive backfield and the timing of plays that an important fact is forgotten, namely, that no offense, or the ballcarriers in it, can be any better than the blocking that team is capable of carrying out. Poor blocking will not open any holes, regardless of how well the offensive men who can delay the defensive pass rush, and no quarterback or ballcarrier will achieve success consistently unless he has both the time and the opportunity to exhibit his skills. A good line not only forces the defense to play the inside option, but also creates situations favouring runs to the outside and play-action passing.

Recognizing the defense

Generally, when coaches talk about reading defenses, they are referring to the quarterback's ability to recognize the defensive formation and the type of coverage used in the secondary. Less well understood is the fact that all offensive players, including linemen, must be able to read defenses to a certain extent.

There are three general types of defenses: the five-man front with a four-deep secondary and two inside linebackers, and an overshifted front, which may use a combination of the previous two. The "three-man front" seen in professional football is actually a five-man front in which the defensive ends serve as outside linebackers.

Certain aspects of defensive coverage of the triple option remain constant regardless of the formation used. There must be a defensive back on each side (the safeties in Figure 1) to take the ends in the deep third of the field. If the offensive team is in a wishbone set, the defense will have to deploy two defensive backs. If the offensive team is in an I or veer set, the defense will need three defensive backs. The defense will have to assign players (the tackles) to make the dive back on the dive play on each side of the line of scrimmage. Players (defensive ends) on either side of the defensive line must be responsible for the quarterback when he turns upfield. There must be defensive players on each side (the cornerbacks) who are responsible for the pitch man on the pitch option from the quarterback.

Thus, the triple option play can serve to force as

many as eight defensive players to maintain their positions in order to cover the option play. The coach can change players' individual responsibilities concerning particular offensive players, but he cannot change any part of his basic coverage and still provide the kind of defensive coverage necessary to adequately defense the triple option. The defense is more or less forced to deploy a basic alignment resembling that shown in Figure 1.

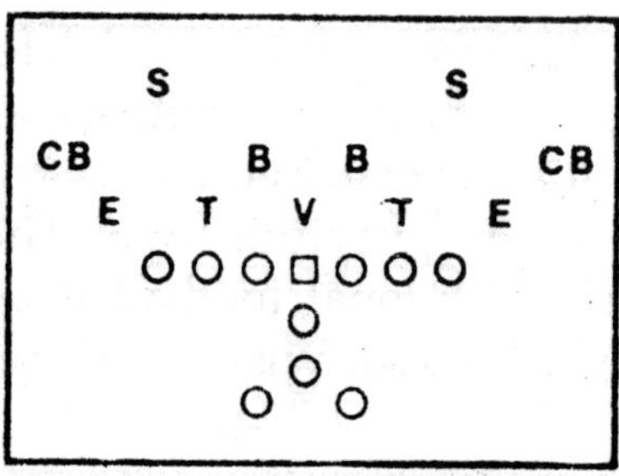

FIG. 2: Odd—front Defense

The positions taken by the three defensive players who are not assigned to one of the eight specific areas previously mentioned will determine which type of defensive system they are playing. The offense will then be able to identify the defense as even-or odd-front. A defense is referred to as odd-front when it has someone playing directly in front of the offensive center. Odd-front alignments generally feature five defensive linemen, including a noseman head up on the center and two defensive tackles playing anywhere from head up to the outside shoulder of the offensive tackle, depending upon coaching preferences. The two defensive ends assume a two-point stance outside the widest offensive lineman (the offensive tackle or the tight end), while the two inside linebackers play head up on the offensive guards and two to three yards off the line of scrimmage. Defenses are called even-front when they do not have a player lined up in front of the center. Usually, this involves some type of six-man line.

There are numerous looks and variations a defense can give to an even front. One of the most commonly encountered variations has the guards playing on the inside shoulders of the offensive guards, the two defensive tackles playing on the outside shoulders (or in the outside gap) of the offensive tackles, and the defensive ends playing outside the tight ends in a two-point stance. In the event that there is no tight end on one side, the defensive end will close down toward the center and play the offensive tackle as he would play the tight end. The two inside linebackers will play two to three yards off the line and on the inside shoulders of the offensive tackles.

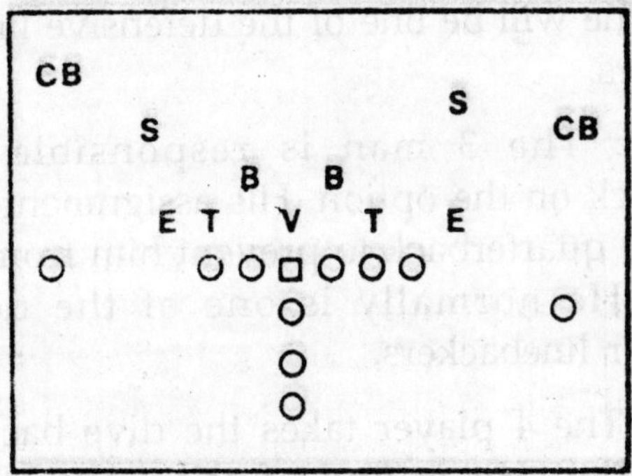

FIG. 3: One type of overshifted front

Overshifted fronts have many different variations, but all variations retain eight people in the basic areas to defense the triple option. The defensive shift is used either to confuse the offense, or to get more defenders into a particular area of strength in the offensive system. Overshifted fronts are most effective against offenses that show strong tendencies to run in designated areas—for example, running behind an outstanding lineman in short—yardage situations.

The defenders can be numbered to help offensive players in their blocking assignments. The defense is always numbered from the outside toward the center. Therefore, the players in the deep one-third of the field on each side will be the 1 defender, the next player will be 2, etc.

1 player: In the defensive secondary, the 1 player is the player on each side of the field who is assigned the deep one third of the field toward the sideline.

2 player: The 2 man is the defense player responsible for the pitch man in the triple option. He may be a defensive back in some defenses, and in others he will be one of the defensive linemen or linebackers.

3 player: The 3 man is responsible for the quarterback on the option. His assignment involves taking the quarterback to prevent him from turning upfield. He normally is one of the defensive linemen or linebackers.

4 player: The 4 player takes the dive back on the option play. He is one of the down linemen, usually a defensive guard or tackle, depending upon the defensive set.

This method, or any of several variations commonly encountered, helps to assure that offensive players know who they are supposed to block.

Defenses will try to camouflage their coverage until the last possible moment, which means that offensive players must be assigned areas rather than specific defenders in their blocking assignments.

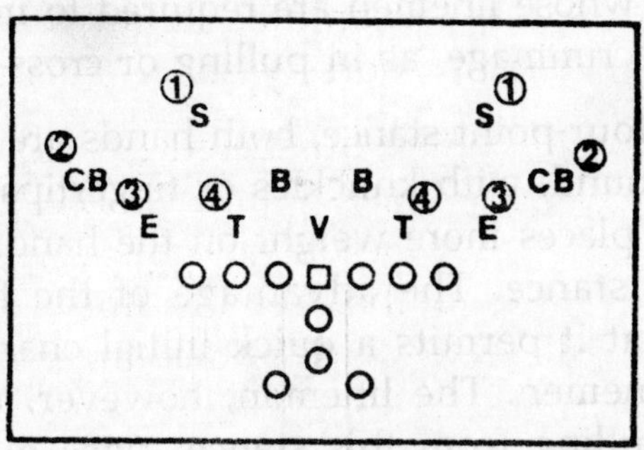

FIG. 4: Numbering the defensive keys

The rational underlying the use of specific types of defensive coverage that affect numbering systems, "Defensive Concepts and Option Football."

Stance

The two basic stances used on the offensive line are the three-and four-point stances. In both stances, the offensive lineman's head should be turned upward, with his eyes directed straight ahead and his shoulders parallel to the line of scrimmage. His feet should be pointed straight ahead at slightly more than shoulder-width apart. His head should be up, and his back as straight as possible. His feet should be nearly flat on the ground.

In the three-point stance one foot is slightly ahead of the other, with the right hand (assuming the player is right-handed) placed on the ground with knuckles or fingertips touching the ground. The other arm is normally placed on the player's knee. The lineman must have enough of his body weight on his hand to be able to charge forward out of his stance, but not so much that he will be unable to pull and move down the line of scrimmage. The three-point stance is used with teams whose linemen are required to move along the line of scrimmage, as in pulling or cross-blocking.

In the four-point stance, both hands are in contact with the ground, with knuckles or fingertips touching. This stance places more weight on the hands than the three-point stance. The advantage of the four-point stance is that it permits a quick initial charge by the offensive linemen. The lineman, however, may have difficulty pulling from this stance, since most of his body weight is forward. He will also have trouble making any type of cross or trap block. When teaching young linemen to assume a correct stance, it is important to remember that individual stances may vary somewhat, but can move out of it quickly.

Drive blocking

The drive block is used to forcibly drive a defensive lineman from the ballcarrier's designated path. This is the most important block in non-option football, and is important to option teams as well, since no team runs triple option every play. To drive block the defensive lineman to his right, the offensive lineman should step up with his near foot and drive the point of his right shoulder into the defensive lineman's beltline. He should keep his head up at all times during the block to help avoid a neck injury. His head should be between the ballcarrier and the defensive lineman. Both of his forearms should be held high with the hands turned in toward the body, in order to widen the blocking surface and keep the defensive lineman from sliding to one side and beating the block. Keeping the hands turned in also will help eliminate holding penalties.

The offensive lineman should follow through with quick, short steps, forceful leg drive, and feet spread wide throughout the block. Quick steps will help the offensive lineman maintain balance and contact with the defensive lineman.

DOUBLE-TEAMING

Double-teaming consists of two offensive linemen working against one defensive lineman. Double-teaming occurs frequently in the triple option series, with the center and guard doubling on the noseman. The blocker directly in front of the defensive lineman is called the post man, and the blocker who forces the defensive lineman to one side is called the drive blocker. The post man should contact the defensive lineman at waist level or lower, with the drive blocker's contact occurring in the defender's rib cage area. The post man should take short, choppy steps and execute his part of the block as if he were using a drive block. The drive blocker takes longer steps initially than the post man, but after solid contact has been made and the defensive lineman has been turned, he (the drive blocker) should take quick short steps.

Double-teaming normally is a very effective type of blocking. In addition to its triple option usage, double-teaming is used in connection with trap blocking on conventional plays. The defensive lineman playing inside the lineman being trapped will be the defender who is double-teamed.

Cross-body block

Cross-body blocks are used not to move defensive linemen, but to cut off their pursuit in a particular direction. Cross-body blocks are normally used against defensive linemen playing outside the blocker. In order to cross-body block the defensive lineman to his right, the offensive lineman should lead with his right foot with his body low and hook his right arm and shoulder beyond the defensive lineman's right leg. After stepping with this left foot, the blocker should throw his left leg against the defender's legs, and he should try to raise his hips to throw the defender off balance. The offensive lineman should follow through by keeping his hands and feet propelling him into the defensive lineman's body. The blocker should maintain contact with the defender until he hears the whistle stopping the play.

Pulling

Offensive linemen should be able to pull in order to execute a good cross block or trap block, and to get outside the defensive end to act as lead blocker for the ballcarrier. The pulling lineman's start involves several movements. First, he simultaneously twists and thrusts his upper body, head and arms toward the side to which he is pulling, allowing the arm to the side he is pulling to whip his body around. He also pivots on the ball of his back foot and takes a short step parallel to the line of scrimmage with his lead foot. His next step is taken with it is directed away from the line of scrimmage to clear the feet of the offensive lineman next to him in the direction he is pulling. The pulling lineman is then in a position to move down the line until he is ready to turn upfield into the line or beyond the defensive end.

Cross blocking

Cross blocking is used primarily in cases in which two offensive linemen have defenders playing nearly head up on them and neither of the offensive linemen has a good blocking angle. By cross blocking to change defensive assignments, both offensive linemen will have a good angle from which to create and attack an opening in the defensive line. The linemen should be in a three-point stance, since they will move parallel to the line of scrimmage. If one of the defenders is playing on the line and the other is playing slightly off the line (e.g., a defensive tackle and a linebacker), the offensive lineman who has to make the block on the line moves first and should lead with the foot on the side to which he is going. He should keep his head between the defender and the hole. The second lineman should step as if pulling with the foot on the side to which he is moving to make his block. He moves down the line of scrimmage until he clears his team-mate, then turns up and executes a shoulder block on the defender he is assigned to. He also should keep his head between the defender and the ballcarrier. The blocker's movement prevents the defender from sliding off the block and making the play on the ballcarrier.

Seal block

This type of block is used when an lineman wants to get in front of the defender and prevent him from moving down the line of scrimmage. The offensive lineman should position his body directly in front of the defender and meet him head on. The blocker holds his forearms high, with his hands turned in toward his body. He contacts the defender about waist high and straightens him up. The blocker should keep his body squared to the defender and use short, quick steps in order to maintain his balance, move with the defender, and stay in front of him.

Open-field blocking

One of the most important aspects of option football is open-field blocking. Every offensive play, regardless of the system used, is designed to get the ballcarrier beyond the line of scrimmage. It is at this point in the game, when the ballcarrier reaches the defensive secondary, that he can put his speed and skills to utmost use. The more blocks a ballcarrier receives beyond the line of scrimmage, the more effective his running will be. Offensive linemen who do not have a key block in the play are usually given the assignment of releasing to block downfield.

The ballcarrier can be of great help to the offensive blocker by setting up his blocks. He can do this in a variety of ways—for example, by "staying in the blocker's hip pocket," by forcing the defensive player to commit to his (the ballcarrier's) movements, or by cutting directly toward the defensive player and "freezing" him so the blocker can more easily perform his assignment.

Through constant drills and practice, the blocker already known the approximate path that the ballcarrier will take, and attempts to position himself between the ballcarrier and the defensive player. When the blocker finds himself having to block a defender in the open field, he should always keep his head up, his eyes open, and his feet far enough apart to maintain a balanced stance. The key to any open-field block is getting close to the defender before committing to any course of action. The defender then has less opportunity to know what type of block the blocker will use.

Run-through block

In open field, most defenders try to keep blockers from reaching their bodies. The blocker's task, then, is to find a way to get to the defender's body with a hand check or forearm shiver. Thus, the blocker will want to start his block beneath the defender's hands and drive up into his body to stop his movement. The forearms and hands should be carried as in drive blocking. It is extremely important that the blocker keep his eyes open and his head up, anticipating the defender's trying to prevent him from getting to his (the defender's) body. The blocker must also be alert for any last-second changes in the defender's position. His head should be turned to the side he expects the ballcarrier to cut to. Once the blocker gets close to the defensive player, he should shorten his stride to bring his body under control and keep his leg drive to maintain contact with the defensive player.

Three other types of open-field blocks—the roll black, the reverse body block and the (open-filed) cross-body block—are all variations of the same principle, that of getting the blocker's entire body in front of the defender. Such blocks are used primarily against defensive backs, but they can be used in cutting off linebackers and defensive ends from their pursuit angles.

Roll blocking

In roll blocking, the blocker approaches the defensive player in an aggressive manner, as if using a run-through block, but as he near the defensive player he throws his arms and upper body downward and drives his hips into the upper portion of the defender's legs. The blocker should land on his hands and feet, and roll his entire body into the defender by whipping his legs body into him and rolling after him if he tried to retreat or elude the block.

Reverse body block

In roll blocking, the blocker leads with his head in the direction he is running; in the reverse body block, the opposite is true. The blocker approaches the defender as in the roll block. As he reaches the defender, however, the blocker whips his legs around and toward the defender. In effect, he is leading with his legs rather than his head. This action will generate a great deal of initial momentum. If the block is executed correctly, it will, at the very least, force the defender off-balance. The blocker should land on all fours and, using his hands and arms, continue to move into the defender's body until the ballcarrier can make his cut past the defensive player.

Cross-body block-open field

Open-field cross-body blocks will normally occur when the blocker and the defensive player are moving at right angles to one another—for example, the lead blocker in a wishbone set and the defensive cornerback. The blocker should be within four feet of the defender when he starts his movement. He plants his lead foot and drives his entire body into the defender at belt level, landing on all fours and finishing the block in the same manner as a reverse body block.

THE TIGHT END POSITION

The tight end has three basic skills that he must accomplish. He must be able to work himself open, catch the football, and block.

Stance

The tight end must block on the line of scrimmage. Therefore, he needs a balanced stance which will allow him to move in any direction. At various times he will be required: to release downfield on a defensive back; to turn out on the defensive end; to block down on the tackle; and, occasionally, to release down on the inside linebacker. In order to perform these different types of blocks, the tight end assumes a stance resembling that of an offensive lineman rather than that of a wide receive. The tight end normally lines up in a three-point stance.

The tight end's feet should be approximately shoulder-width evenly on both feet, with very little weight resting on his hands. His head should remain up, his eyes looking straight ahead so he can see the defense without tipping off the direction of his release.

The defense may use a defensive player—a defensive end or linebacker—to try to delay the tight end from releasing quickly. If the defensive end is given this responsibility, he will normally try to force the tight end back toward the middle by using his inside forearm. The linebacker uses either a forearm or hand shiver to slow the tight end and delay him from completing his assignment. The defense may use this tactic to prevent the tight end from moving downfield to block on the defensive back, or to throw him off-stride and reduce the effectiveness of blocks on the line of scrimmage. The tight end must then be ready to use fakes or evasive actions to get away from the defensive player trying to delay him at the line of scrimmage. The most common action is to take a jab-step in one direction and then release in another direction. The tight end may also fake a block, slide off, and release.

Blocking

The tight end must be versatile to perform all of his duties well. He is responsible for a variety of blocking actions and assignments. Different triple option formations may require him to perform several different types of blocks in the course of a game.

Many of the blocks executed by the tight end occur at the line of scrimmage. In order to keep the defense off-balance and unable to read the play until the last moment, teams often use different assignments on the same play against the same defensive alignment.

The tight end executes drive blocks as described previously. He normally drive blocks on a defensive end who has been crashing into the offensive backfield in an attempt to destroy the timing of the option play. The tight end should turn out on the defensive end with his head to the inside of the defender's body, and thus force the defensive end to go around his block and delay his entry into the backfield.

If the linebacker has been consistently beating the offensive tackle's block on the option play, the tight end may perform a seal block in either of two ways. First, he may step across the line of scrimmage and square up to the linebacker with feet spread, knees bent, forearms up, and hands turned into his body. He is now in position to react to the linebacker as he comes down the line of scrimmage pursuing the option play. The tight end should maintain his balance, and not lunge at the linebacker and try to slow down his pursuit. He should use proper form and technique primarily rather than strength in executing this block, staying between the linebacker and the outside area he wishes to protect.

The second type of block that the tight end can use to seal the linebacker to the inside is the cross-body block. This type of block can be extremely effective if used sparingly. The linebacker will have his attention focused on the offensive backfield, depending upon his peripheral vision to alert him to offensive players trying to block him. Therefore, he will not be able to pick up the tight end's block as quickly as that of an offensive player directly in front of him. The tight end should execute the cross-body block as described previously.

Sometimes the tight end will have to block the defensive tackle. Since the tackle normally plays inside the tight end, all the end will be able to do is either drive the tackle down the line toward the center or use a cut-off block to stop his penetration. The former technique, that of the tight end driving the tackle down the line, is performed like the first part of the cross-block between two linemen. The tight end carries out his part of the block just as the offensive lineman who moves first in the normal cross block. The offensive tackle may or may not carry out the other part of the block, depending upon whether the defensive tackle is being double-teamed. When the right end uses a cut-off block on the defensive tackle, he should try to get his head and upper body in front of the tackle at about knee level. He should be on all fours, and then raise his body and maintain contact with the defensive player. This block may not bring the tackle off his feet, but it should serve to stop his forward penetration if executed properly.

The tight end has several options available in carrying out his assignment whenever he releases downfield to block one of the defensive backs. He will probably start with the "run-off" technique. The tight end starts downfield toward the defensive back, and as long as the defensive back goes with him and does not stop or come up to give run support, it is not necessary to block him. The tight end will merely sprint downfield and take the defensive back out of the play.

If the defensive back does not retreat, however, or if he allows the tight end to get too close to him, the end should use a roll, reverse-body, or cross-body, whichever the end is in position to execute, to take the defensive back out of the play. It the defensive back retreats and then either starts to break down or come up to play the run, the tight end should block him immediately, using any of the aforementioned open-field blocks.

Defenses use different types of secondary coverage during the game. The tight end should know his numbering rules, since he will probably be assigned a number rather than a particular player. That way, even if the defense changes the run, the tight end should have no real problem knowing which player to block.

FLANKERS AND SPLIT ENDS

Split ends and flankers should start from three-point stances, but their stances differ greatly from the tight end's three-point stance. Wide-out receivers do not need a balanced stance, since they will move straight ahead for at least their first couple of steps, with no side-to-side movement. They should assume sprinters' stances in order to move downfield as quickly as possible. Placing one foot behind the other will give most players a faster start.

Wide receivers do not usually have much trouble releasing from the line of scrimmage due to their position on the field, and because there are fewer defenders around them to delay their release. The wide-out should release at the same rate of speed, and in the same manner, on each play. If the receiver uses different releases on different plays, defensive backs will soon pick up the cues to read his intentions. If he starts each play the same way, he forces the defender to play him honestly. His first steps should remain the same whether the play is a run or a pass. When the defender releases off the line, the wide receiver should run directly at the defender. This move serves to slow the defender's reading of the play, and may give the receiver a slight advantage if he is running a pass route.

The wide receiver does not have to block on the line of scrimmage. The only block he will be required to make is an open-field block. The faster and better receiver a split end or flanker is, the more effective he will find the run-off technique, since the secondary defenders may need a large cushion between themselves and the receivers. The run-off technique is described and should be carried out in that manner by the wide-out receiver. On plays in which the wide-out has to block, he should use whichever open-field block he is in position to perform. Faking ability is an essential skill for any receiver, regardless of his position. A receiver who makes good use of fakes can compensate to some extent for a lack of speed. The purpose of faking is to get as much distance as possible between the receiver and the defensive back covering him. This is accomplished by confusing the defender as to which route the receiver is running, or by making the defender commit himself in the wrong direction.

The receiver can create distance between himself and the defender in any of several ways. He may take a step and turn his body in one direction, then cut off the same foot in another direction, hoping the defender will react to the first action and be off-balance when he starts into his route. He may start on one route, and then break off into another route—for example, starting a sideline route and then turning upfield on a deep route, catching the defender with his momentum toward the line of scrimmage. He may use a change of pace to slow the defender down, and resume full speed before the defender can react. Or he may use his hands and eyes to simulate trying for the reception, then beat the defender on a deeper route.

Getting open is only the first part of a receiver's assignment on passing downs. The most important part is catching the ball. The receiver's hands should make first contact with the ball, and his arms should act as a cushion for the thumbs out, which softens the impact between ball and hands. The fingers adjust to, and give with, the ball more easily than the thumbs. This method can be used with passes that are not in a direct line with the receiver's body.

On deep routes, the receiver can usually adjust his body to use the thumbs-out position. The receiver has less opportunity to adjust to the ball on short routes, and often must catch it the best way he can. If the pass is to the inside and he cannot use the thumbs-out method, the receiver has two choices: he can use the thumbs-in technique, or he can try to catch the point of the ball with one hand and the side of the ball with the other hand.

With the thumbs inside, the receiver has less flexibility and "give" with his hands. Some coaches fear that, when the receiver tries to catch the pass with his hands on the sides of the ball, the will slip through the gap between his hands if he doesn't close his hands at exactly the right moment. Concerning the latter alternative, catching the point of the ball with one hand and the side of the ball with the other, the ball has less chance of getting by the receiver and being intercepted, and since the ball usually stays in front of the receiver he may have another opportunity to grab for it. By keeping the elbows close together, the receiver is less likely to have the ball slide through his arms.

Forward passing techniques have evolved to the extent that quarterbacks often release the ball before the receiver even begins to make his break. Thus, it is important for the receiver to turn his head and locate the ball as quickly as possible, since the longer he is able to see the ball in flight, the better his chances will be of catching it. It becomes even more important to see the ball quickly on poorly thrown passes, since the receiver has to adjust his path to the ball.

QUARTERBACKS

Many non-option plays feature the quarterback's either handing off deep in the backfield, or turning and making the pitch while the runner is four to six yards deep in the backfield. Deep handoffs enable the ballcarrier to read the blocks and choose his opening along the line of scrimmage—and with an outstanding runner in the backfield unencumbered by having to follow a predetermined route, the advantages can be considerable. On the other hand, the running back must be capable if the deep pitch is to succeed, since his position in the backfield means that the defense will have more time to react to his movements than if he were receiving a quick handoff. Furthermore, not only does the runner receive the ball four to six yards deep in the backfield when the pitch is made early, but he is inside the defensive containment (i.e., the defensive ends) when he receives the ball.

In the triple option play, the quarterback reads openings along the line, which means that the running backs are relieved of this responsibility. This was not always the case with option plays. As late as the mid-'60s, many coaches used their fullback to read the inside option. If he saw an opening in the defense's inside coverage, the fullback wrenched the ball away from the quarterback's hands and carried the ball himself. If he saw that the dive route as covered, however, he permitted the quarterback to pull the ball away and continue down the line for the outside option. Most option coaches have since gone away from this technique, however, for three reasons. First, having two players holding onto the ball at the same time is far more likely to produce fumbles than having the quarterback hold the ball and the fullback form a pocket for the quarterback to insert the ball in. Second, the quarterback is in a better position to read the defense than the fullback—his stance is erect and stationary (momentarily) at the mesh point, while the fullback is in a low stance, leaning forward and running at full speed toward the line. Finally, while training a quarterback to read the defense and make correct option decisions is difficult and time-consuming, it is easier in terms of teamwork and timing to teach one player to make all the decisions than to parcel out the responsibilities among two or more players.

Thus, the quarterback is responsible for making the choices designed to place the eventual ballcarrier in an opening in, or outside, the defensive line. Regardless of which option the quarterback selects, the runner will be close to the line of scrimmage when he receives the ball.

In learning to run the triple option, the quarterback must first learn to take the snap and get into his mesh with the dive back. The laces of the ball should always be under the fingers of the quarterback's throwing hand, with that hand slightly back of the middle of the ball.

The quarterback should take his first step to the side of the play at the same instant the center begins his snap. He should not wait until the ball is in his hands. The quarterback must maintain a firm grip on the ball. If he tries to hold the ball in one hand, or relaxes his grip, the ball may be knocked out of his hands. The quarterback rides the dive back into the line of scrimmage—that is, he attempts to place the ball into the dive back's pocket as quickly as possible, and leave if there until the last second. The longer the quarterback can maintain the ride, the more time he will have to force defenders to commit to the dive back and leave themselves vulnerable to the outside option. The quarterback should step up into the line with the dive back in order to hold the linebackers insides as long as possible. If the defense does not play the dive back, the quarterback leaves the ball with him and continues down the line, faking the outside option. When the defense commits to the dive back, the quarterback pulls the ball out of the dive back's pocket, steps behind him and continues the option to the defensive end.

Once the quarterback pulls the ball out of the dive back's pocket, he should immediately bring the ball to the middle of his chest with both hands. He is now in position to throw the ball quickly, and he has excellent control of the ball even if he doesn't pass the ball.

The moment the ball is snapped, the quarterback should start looking for his defensive key, the defender assigned responsibility for the dive back. The instant he takes the ball away from the dive back, the quarterback should immediately pick up his second key to watch his reactions to the play. If the defensive key—normally the defensive end—takes the pitch man and the quarterback turns upfield, he should tuck the ball away with the point of the ball in the palm of his outside hand and away from the defensive pursuit. The other end of the ball should be locked under his arm to avoid fumbling when he is tackled. If the quarterback has to option the ball off to the pitch man, having the ball in the middle of his chest and holding it with both hands will give him better control of the ball prior to the pitch.

In passing, the ball is held with the laces under the fingers, and the index and middle fingers off the laces and toward the end of the ball. Holding the ball behind the middle gives the pass more spiral, and thus greater accuracy. The ball should be held firmly, but not too tightly, in both hands just beneath the chin and toward the shoulder of the passing arm. The throwing hand should be brought directly back from that point, and not dropped down as in throwing a baseball. This motion affords the quarterback a quicker release, and permits him to hold onto the ball until the last second.

Once the quarterback locates his receiver, he is ready to throw the ball. His weight should be resting on his right foot if he is a right-handed passer. As his arm starts forward, he should take a short step with his left foot. His left toe should be pointed toward the receiver. The ball is thrown with an overhand motion that carries the ball close to the passer's ear.

The quarterback's wrist should be cocked as he brings the ball back tilted slightly up and pointed downfield. The passing arm should end of the throw. The ball rolls off the fingertips as the ball is released, with the index finger being the last part of the hand to leave the ball. The arm follows through, with the palm turning outward at the end of the throwing action.

If the quarterback has to throw on the run, he should square his shoulders to the line of scrimmage before passing. The passer should avoid throwing away from the direction in which he is moving. When throwing the ball on the run, it is necessary for him to increase his wrist action, since he is not set to throw with proper follow-through.

DIVE BACKS

Dive backs play in different positions, according to the offensive alignment being used. The wishbone fullback normally assumes a four-point stance. His feet should be nearly parallel, with no more than a heel-to-toe relationship. Both hands should be touching the ground, with more body weight resting on his hands than would be the case in a three-point stance. This limits the fullback's lateral movement, but gives him a quicker, more powerful charge than other stances. Wishbone fullbacks move straight ahead in most cases, with a minimum of lateral movement in their initial burst.

The fullback's first step should be with the foot to the side of the play. The step should be relatively short, with the back foot pushing off to build up force and momentum. The fullback needs a good start because normally he is closer to the line in the wishbone than dive backs in the other option sets. At his first step he should begin to raise the arm on the quarterback turns to put the ball in the pocket. His other arm should be carried lower (at waist level), with palm upturned.

When the fullback feels the ball, he rolls his shoulder downward to hide the ball but does not grasp it. He only wants to feel the ball, not take it away from the quarterback. The quarterback should be able to pull the ball out if the defensive key takes the fullback.

If the ball is given to him, the fullback should either keep both hands over it or tuck the ball away. If the ball is taken away, the fullback must continue as if he had the ball to confuse the defense as long as possible.

When running in traffic, the ballcarrier should have the ball tucked away. The rear of the ball should be jammed into the armpit and the side of the upper chest. The forearm should be held along, and slightly beneath, the ball so that the ball is held against the side of the body and upper chest. The hand and fingers should be closed over the point of the ball, pulling it back into the upper arm.

When the play is to the right, the ball should be held in the right arm, and in the left arm if the play is to that side. The ides is to have the defenders on the free side of the ballcarrier where they have less chance to make contact with the ball and force a fumble.

On plays in which the ball carrier is running into, or through, the middle of the line, the ball may be carried in front of the body in both arms, giving the ballcarrier maximum protection against fumbles in an area of play in which fumbles are most likely to occur. The ballcarrier's arms should be crossed in front of his body, with one arm on top of, and one arm beneath, the ball. His hands should cover both ends of the ball and, if proper forward body lean is used, his shoulders will help protect him from defenders reaching in and stripping the ball from his grasp.

In order for the option play to succeed, the fullback must be able to carry out his blocking assignment. When the quarterback pulls the ball out of the fullback's pocket, he (the fullback) blocks the defensive key, which is normally the defensive tackle in most defenses. The fullback must ensure that the tackle does not cross the line of scrimmage—an act which can be disastrous to the triple option. The fullback should stay low and reach the defender's lower body to slow him up and reduce his mobility. The fullback also may be expected to block the middle linebacker in some cases—for example, in the isolation play in which the fullback leads the halfback into the hole. The fullback should stay low and get his head on the side of the defensive player that the ballcarrier will be going, in order to keep the defender out of the play. The quarterback normally fakes a handoff to the fullback, which will help with the fullback's block on the linebacker if the fake is executed properly. Once the fullback makers contact, he should use short steps to keep his balance and develop leg drive.

OTHER CONSIDERATIONS FOR RUNNING BACKS

Wishbone halfbacks may use either a two-or three-point stance. In the two-point stance, the halfback rests his hands on his knees, with his weight carried on the bails of his feet. This stance permits him to use lateral movement in either direction, but is slow for straight-ahead play.

The halfback is the lead blocker in the option play, usually blocking a defensive back with one of the open-field blocks described previously. He must be sure make at least partial contact with the defensive player—he doesn't have to block the defender off his feet, and normally he will not. All he really needs to do is screen him away from the ballcarrier.

When the halfback is responsible for blocking the defensive end, he will most likely use a drive or cutoff block, attempting to get his head between the defender and ballcarrier.

The tailback in the formation uses a two-point stance. He must be able to get outside quickly in sweep action, and move parallel to the line so that he gets the ball deep on blast plays. The tailback must be able to find, and cut to, openings along the line of scrimmage. When the ball is snapped, he should begin searching for an opening in the line.

A familiar formation play involves sprint-draw. The tailback moves along the line, paralleling it, and the quarterback gives the ball to him deep in the backfield. The tailback is then given the opportunity to use his cutting ability to move to the hole and his leg drive to break tackles.

A vast difference exists between the power of inside runners, and outside runners who seem to flow by tacklers. Players are no better than their physical abilities allow them to be, but a sound grasp of fundamentals allows a player to most nearly reach his potential. Inside runners use shorter stride than outside runners, and as a result their feet should be farther apart. Shortening his stride slows a runner somewhat, but his running is more balanced and he is harder to bring down. Balance is very important to the inside runner because his running area is so congested. He is likely to bump into both offensive and defensive players, and quick short steps enable him to maintain his balance and make the quick cuts that are so important to inside running. Inside runners should run with their knees bent and their bodies as low as possible. Defensive players will grab at him constantly, and if he has good leg drive he should be able to break many of those tackles.

Outside runners use a longer, more fluid stride than inside runners. They should be able to use at least three basic moves: the side-step, spin-out, and cross-over. In side-stepping a tackler, the runner steps directly toward him with the opposite foot from the hand carrying the ball. His body weight should be kept forward and on his toes. At the moment of contact, the runner takes a wide step away from the defender to the side he is carrying the ball on, and places his weight on that leg. This leaves the original leg limp and free of any weight. Often, the tackler will slide off and lose his grasp of the ballcarrier.

In spinning away from a tackler, the ballcarrier should have a low stance with his weight forward as the defender makes contact, hit the tackler with the shoulder opposite the ball side and spin in the direction of the contact shoulder. His body must be carried low, and he must use leg drive to break the tackle and retain as much of his forward momentum as possible.

In executing a cross-over, the defender should be approached in the same manner as in the side-step, but just before contact occurs, the ballcarrier shifts his weight from the foot in front of the defender is lifted high and swung sharply across the other leg in a cross-over motion.

The outside runner can be a great help to his lead blocker. No runner should feel that, because he is carrying the ball, there should be an enormous hole for him to run through. Getting past defenders is the runner's responsibility as well as that of his blockers. If the runner can he should help set up his blockers by faking, or by positioning himself behind his blocker and the defensive player. Fakes can serve to freeze the defender momentarily, which should enable the blocker to make better contact. The runner's staying behind his blocker will make the defender fight through or around the blocker to get to him.

The ballcarrier should always fight for extra yardage. Even an extra foot or less of yardage can spell the difference between a first down and having to punt. Forward body lean is extremely important. By running low with high leg drive, the ballcarrier provides fewer opportunities for the defense to make solid contact than if he were running in an upright position. A trait shared by all quality runners is the ability to pick up extra yardage after defensive contact has been made.

4 KICKING

KICK WITH INSIDE OF THE FOOT

The kick is not taken for a long distance but pushed for a short distance. This type of kick is most commonly used when the ball is to be played first time and accuracy is more desirable than the speed. In addition, the kick is easy to master. The kick with inside of the foot has disadvantages too. The player cannot kick the ball while running, as he needs to slow down his pace of running, because the horizontal axis of the kicking foot which is pointing forward in the direction of kick must be turned to the side in order to make contact with the ball. However, keeping in view the frequency of execution of the kick in the game, it is necessary to master this technique.

TECHNIQUE OF KICKING WITH INSIDE OF FOOT

To execute the kick with inside of the foot, the approach run should preferably be short and straight to the ball. A longer approach run does not increase the power or speed of the pass, because of the restricted movement of the foot. The most important thing is the rhythm of approach which should not be broken. The last step of approach is adjusted in such a way that it is just like regular running stride which is timed so that it is placed comfortably along side the ball at the time of kick, which should also be shortly bent at the knee joint and should bear the weight of body.

The kicking foot is turned to the side from the hip joint. Thus making an angle of 90 with non kicking foot and is off the ground. The ball is struck in the Centre. Before doing so the foot first is taken back in order to apply force by a vigorous extension of the knee joint and the inside of the foot is driven straight through the centre of the ball. The impact is follow by a long follow through towards the target, which ensures accuracy in the kick.

The arc of the back is not stressed, as in the case of other kicks, for the simple reason that this type of kick is not supposed to be a powerful kick. Rather the body is slightly bent forward in order to bring the knee of the kicking foot over the ball, so that ball is kept low to the target. The body, however, is lifted simultaneously as a counter action of the kicking leg, particular when the kicking leg is following the direction of the kick.

KICK WITH THE FULL INSTEP

Kick with the full instep is also called low drive, which generally is considered to be the most powerful kick because the direction of approach and the direction of intended kick are both identical. The kick with the instep means that the contact with the ball has to be made just above the metatarsal arc with the ankle joint fixed firmly. The kick is taken for short and long distance passes and also for the passes of medium height. Medium height kick can normally be seen at the time of scoring. Kicking with full instep is most powerful and natural kick as it can be carried out without reducing the pace of running and without altering the position of the foot at ankle joint.

TECHNIQUE OF KICKING THE BALL WITH FULL INSTEP

The ball is approached from a distance of 5 to 6 steps in such a manner that the first steps are shorter than the last one. The last longer step provides sufficient time for taking up correct position, and for the back swing of the kicking foot. The perfect timing and exclusive concentration on the ball helps the player in planting the non-kicking foot just along side the ball which generally is 6 to 8 inches away from the ball and pointing towards the direction of kick. Almost at the same time when non-kicking foot is places along side the ball the other leg swings backward. The swing is in the line of the intended kick. This swinging action of the kicking leg from the hop joint is grater than in any other kick. Almost the whole body posture particularly helps in checking the forward momentum and controls the body to gain sufficient time for kicking action. The leg is well-bent at the knee joint which forms an acute angle, thus increasing the arc through which the foot moves. The arm of the non-kicking leg hangs forward while the other arm is somewhere behind the body to maintain balance.

The real kicking starts when swing is followed by the forward swing. This movement starts from hip which pulls the thigh forward abruptly with the intensive movement of the swinging leg forward. With simultaneously counter action of the trunk, during those forward movement, the foot at ankle joint is stretched backward and downward and the impact with the ball is made in the centre. At the time of impact, the knee is kept over the ball. The kicking foot moves through an arc, when the ball beyond the line of the knee. The foot comes into contact with the ball as the arc. This will keep the ball low. In the final stages of the movement the foot follows through in the direction of the kick. The knee straightens and the leg moves forward from the hip joint. Then the knee again is slightly bent to come to the running position.

The area of surface of foot which comes on contact with the ball is comparatively lesser than the inside of the foot kick and the toe of the kicking foot must be kept near the ground. The beginners find it difficult to kick the ball. And also because of the loose or inadequate muscle control, the players fail to stretch the toe completely downwards, try to kick the ball with the inside of the step, by facing the ball almost sideways in the hope of gaining power through pivot. But this has a contrary effect as the same causes them to drag the ball in the pivot and thus putting the pass of the target. Therefore. It is suggested not to teach the skill first when the ball is on the ground, but somewhere in the mid air, so that the feeling of correct surface and required muscle sense is developed. It is also suggested that the skill should only be taught after the kick with the inside of the foot. So that the players have already learnt to adjust with the strides to approach the ball.

KICK WITH THE INSIDE OF INSTEP

Kicking with inside of instep is one of the most widely used kicks and is extremely popular with some of the teams. It can be applied for short passes (chip shop) long cross field passes for clearance and for free kicks etc. Such type of passes are made through the air when there is a danger of interception of passes. The long and high passes also has the advantage of covering the maximum distance in just a movement. It is pointless to drive the ball as far as possible with the hope to retain possession. Therefore, the accuracy of passes should be the primary consideration.

TECHNIQUE TO KICK WITH THE INSIDE OF INSTEP

These types of kicks are taken with the inner surface of the foot stretching from the base of the toe to the inner part of the ankle. More precisely, the curve of the ankle is called the inside of instep. Generally, two types of kicks, namely chip shot and high drive, are executed with inside of the inset. Chip shot is a measured and controlled kick, whereas high drive has unlimited possibilities. In high drive, the approach run is 5 to 6 steps, whereas in chip shop, the approach run is restricted to only 2 to 3 steps, because to execute chip shot, much force is not needed, and moreover, the kick is to be executed quickly. The line of approach in both the cases is angular. The chip shot can also be executed with the straight approach run, but in that case the contact with the ball will be made with the full instep. It the kick is to be taken with the right foot, the approach run must be from the left and vice versa. The angle of approach should not be more than 45. At the time of kicking, the leg on which the body rests is placed laterally, but behind the ball. The position of the toe is pointing somewhat against the direction of kick to facilitate the inside of instep to come in contact. During the preparatory movement, the foot of the standing leg is rolled off over the outer the outer side of the foot sole, thus favouring the shift of the body weight to the body weight to the side of the standing leg. The body momentum is checked simultaneously and automatically during the last step of approach the playing foot is brought into position. The lateral side of the trunk and the direction of kick form an acute angle, which means that the shoulder corresponding to the leg on which the body rests, moves slightly forward, while the other shoulder moves backward. When the kick is to be taken for more height the body should be kept leaning backward. At the time of kicking, swinging of kicking leg, the arm opposite to the kicking leg and slight bend of the standing leg maintain the balance.

The kicking leg is turned outward enough from the hip but also swings backward. With the swinging of the leg from hip the leg is also flung backward from the knee. That movement is followed by a powerful forward swing of the kicking foot. This powerful and energetic forward swing is more pronounced in case of high drive. At the time of contact, the knee remains slightly bent which is fully extended during the follow through, so that the leg swings in a circular manner. The curve of the arc is more pronounced in the final stage, that is follow through. This again is emphasised in case of high drive, whereas the follow through in chip shot is restricted.

The other difference between the two kicks is the point of contact with the ball. In case of chip shot, the contact is made at the bottom of the ball as low as possible. The foot attempts to go as much under the ball as possible and leaves a scar on the ground whereas the contact in case of high drive is slightly below the centre of the ball.

KICKING WITH THE OUTSIDE OF THE FOOT

There has been a great trend in the recent years to develop the technique of passing the ball with the outside of the foot. The reason is that it includes feinting in the passing itself, which is also an essential element in the performance of game. For example, it a player is about to be tackled, in the last moment he flicks the ball to a team-mate and can still continue without breaking his pace. Because of its speedy and deceptive nature, this technique is very effective for advanced football players. On the contrary, passing the ball with the inside of the foot is time consuming. This pass does not require any elaborate preparatory movement before the ball is played. Keeping these advantages in view, it is necessary to master this technique of passing.

TECHNIQUE OF KICKING THE BALL WITH THE OUTSIDE OF THE FOOT

Kicking with the outside of the foot is the only technique where the ball can be approached in different manner for different reasons and aims. For example, in chipping, the ball can be approached straightway angularly, but the aim of putting the ball, that is target, remains the same. In this techniques, if the ball is to be kicked straight forward, the approach run should be angular, and if the aim is to kick a swerving ball, the approach run adopted is straight approach, it is difficult to turn the foot inward sufficiently to make an angle of 90 with the foot and the direction of intended kick. The angle of foot and direction of kick is therefore acute. The foot makes contact with the ball slightly to the side of the centre of the ball and the ball swerves. But in angular approach, the angle between the intended direction and the foot is of 90 just like push pass; thus the ball is struck in the middle; therefore, there is no spinning of the ball, but it travels straight.

The distance between the placement of the non-kicking foot and the ball is somewhat greater as compared to other kicks. Greater emphasis is laid on the approach run when it is angular, because the kicking leg is to be turned inward from the hip joint. Therefore, one must have sufficient room for smooth action. The upper part of the body inclines slightly forward on the non-kicking foot. Back swing of the kicking leg in case of straight approach is backward but somewhat to the out. With the beginning of the forward swing the ankle joint stars turning inside and downward as much as ankle joint allows. The shin is thurst towards the ball, but the foot comes in contact with the ball at the desired point.

The final stage of the kicking is finished with following the ball through sufficiently. After driving the ball forward, the kicking leg is straightened and swings across in front of body from the hip while the foot following the upper part of body continues to move backward. But these tendencies can only be described when kicking a stationary ball.

KICKING WITH TOE AND HEEL

With the development of football techniques, the importance of the kick with toe has gradually diminished, and this is considered to be old fashioned type kick, whereas kicking with heel is not a survivor from the past age but has come into being in the modern game. However, both are grouped as an emergency kick and are used less frequently. But under certain circumstances, it is perfectly correct to kick the ball with the toe or heel. For example, if a player is not close enough to the ball, the only alternative is to push the leg forward from the hip and touch the ball only with the toe. Passing with the heel has an advantage of playing the ball back or to the side without turning or pivoting on the standing leg.

TECHNIQUE OF KICKING THE BALL WITH TOE AND HEEL

In heel kick, the standing leg is about one foot in front and to the side of the ball. The toe is pointing against the direction of the kick. In toe kick standing leg almost is identical to the push pass with the foot pointing in the direction of kick. The toe of kicking foot in heel kick is turned upward in such a way that it is parallel to the ground. The initial forward swing of the leg means it overlaps to the side of standing leg slightly bent at knee, and then follows a jerking back swing of lower leg in the knee joint. While kicking the ball with toe, the playing leg is lifted and much bent at knee joint that is initial or preparatory movement for the kick, as the actual kick is performed with complete stretching of the knee joint. Contact in both the cases is made in the middle of the ball with toe and heel respectively. The trunk action is contrary to each other. In kicking with the heel, the upper part of body is much bent forward, whereas in kicking with the toe, the upper part of body is leaning backward.

VOLLEY KICKS

Within the categories of techniques of kicking, volley constitute a separate chapter of paramount importance. This type of kick is made by kicking the ball when it is still in the air Volley kicks can be taken by any part of the foot. But volley kicks executed with the full instep, inside of the foot, and out side of the foot are quite common. Necessity to play the ball in the air arises when a player does not have sufficient time or space to bring the ball under control. This type of kick can also be used for scoring a goal, as it has tremendous advantage of not giving much time to the goalkeeper to save a goal. The types of volley kicks are:

a. Front Volley; b. Volley to the side; c.Overhead kick; d. Overhead kick with falling; e. Scissor kick

FRONT VOLLEY

The elevation and direction of the kick is determined by the height of the ball when played and the body position. The other factor which influences the kick is follow through. If the ball is to be kicked low, the fundamental principles of low drive or kicking with full instep are to be followed. But if the ball is to be kicked high, the toe of the kicking foot will not be perpendicularly downward, but the toe of the foot has to be adjusted according to the flight at which the ball is to be dispatched. In this case, the knee of the kicking foot will not be over the ball.

SIDE VOLLEY

In match there are numerous situations when a player has to kick the approaching ball from the side (ways) and out from the front. For e.g., a ball coming to a forward player from cross pass or a corner kick or a winger has centred the ball and a defender kicks the ball for clearance. In this case, the leg swings forward across the body. The kicking foot in this case is pointing outward to get the contact with the ball. The most important fundamental in this kick is that the player should simultaneously pivot on the standing leg to allow the kicking foot to follow the direction of the kick.

OVERHEAD VOLLEY

In the case of overhead kick, the standing leg is

bending backward and with simultaneous action the playing leg is moved upward to meet the ball high, at least shoulder high. The instep comes in contact with the ball (in front of the ball). The trunk leans backward very much to support the upward action of the kicking leg.

OVERHEAD VOLLEY WITH FALLING

The course of movement of the overhead kick with falling corresponds to the overhead kick except the strong backward lean of the upper part of the body is emphasised so that the contact with the ball can be made at still greater height, in order to put the ball on his back for low pass or for scoring. In this way, the contact with the instep is made just above the middle of the ball. Because of the greater lowering of the trunk to the back, the player falls back. While falling back, both the arms are kept to the side of the body and touch the ground first to cushion the impact.

SCISSOR KICK

The peculiarity of a scissor kick is that the jumping leg or take off leg is also the playing leg. The kick is applied when the player has to jump towards the ball in order to get the ball earlier. To be able to pass the ball low or to score, the knee must be above the ball. Mostly the kick is executed with instep.

HALF VOLLEY

The difference between the volley kick is that, in volley kick, the ball is to be played in the air. But in half volley, the ball is played when it is bouncing from the ground after falling from air. The impact of the ball with ground and the impact of the foot with the ball are simultaneous. It means the ground, ball and kicking foot meet simultaneously. Like low drive, in half volley too, if the ball is to be played for lower height, then the non-kicking foot is to be kept along side the ball. Body and knee are kept over the ball directly. Toe of the kicking foot is well extended downward. But to make lofted half volley, the non-kicking foot is kept behind the ball. So that when the kick is made, the body is leaning backward and the knee is behind the ball, and kicking foot is making upward progress. For accuracy and power, the kick with the inside of the foot and kick with full instep respectively are preferred.

5

OFFENSE

Offensive information and procedures must be organized in such a way that they quickly and clearly communicate to the players. A quarterback cannot come into the huddle and make lengthy, wordy calls. A series of numbers indicating various functions is the quickest means of communication. Some words may have to be used, but coaches must work at keeping play calling *brief. The* quarterback will have to communicate all or some of the following elements in his play call: 1) hole, 2) ball carrier, 30 formation, 4) series, 5) shift, 6) motion, 7) snap count, and 8) break huddle signal. There are many ways in which this can be done. The following is one excellent way.

PLAY CALLING

Hole

Each point of attack along the line of scrimmage should be assigned a number. How they are numbered is immaterial as long as everyone understands the numbering system. Some coaches number offensive players while others prefer to number the holes *between* offensive players.

Ball carrier

Each backfield person should be assigned a number.

Formations

Each formation should be assigned a number. Some coaches use colours.

1. (Blue) I-wing right
2. (Red) I-wing left
3. (Green) Winged- T right
4. (Black) Winged-T left
5. (Gray) Pro right
6. (Brown) Pro left
7. (Purple) Divide, wing right
8. (White) Divide, wing left

These three essential numbers (Hole, ball carrier, formation) can be combined into a number between 111 and 999 that readily indicates all three functions. The formation could be the hundreds number, the ball carrier the tens number, and the hole the units number. Then 324 would mean a play run from the 300 formation, by the 2 back at the 4 hole.

If the second (tens) digit is higher than four (not a back number), it designates a passing series. Five (5) could mean drop back; six (6) sprint out; seven (7) screen; and so on. The third number rather than designating the hole would indicate pass routes. The number 654 could mean a drop back pass from the 600 formation with everyone hooking.

Series

Most teams will attack a hole with a given back in more than one manner. Therefore a word is added either before or after the three numbers indicating the type of play.

Shift

In order to confuse defenses many teams like to shift prior to final alignment. This could easily be indicated by a number preceding the play. For example: 5-324 Trap might mean that the team would initially line up in a 500 formation, shift to the 300 formation on signal, and then run the play.

Motion

Letters of the alphabets can indicate types of motion. A flanker in long motion could be called "x"; a wing in short motion could be called "y"; a TB in motion strong could be called "z". This letter would follow a shift call, but precede the play.

Snap count

This is designated by the QB in the huddle. Some teams utilize a system whereby the ball carrier's number is always the one on which the ball is snapped. This can eliminate one call by the QB in the huddle but prevents the QB from using delayed and quick calls when advisable.

Break

A team should break from the middle uniformly and with enthusiasm. This is best accomplished by having the QB give a break signal at which time everyone claps his hands, yells "break", and moves to the line of scrimmage.

To review the sequence of a play call:

Ist Number indicating pre-shift formation

2nd Letter indicating motion

3rd Hundreds number indicating formation

4th Tens number indicating ball carrier

5th Units number indicating the hole

6th Word indicating series

7th Snap count

8th Break signal

Huddle and break

There are many forms of huddles. Whatever their formation, it is important that all team members can hear the call, that the opposition can't hear the call, and that the huddle facilitates rapid release to the line of scrimmage.

The centre forms the huddle. He should get in a position 7-10 yards behind the spot where the referee has placed the ball. The huddle should look orderly. Football is a game that requires precision and this begins in the huddle.

Some teams allow the centre and wide receivers to leave the huddle early after they have picked up all necessary information. The centre must take his position quickly since other linemen get their splits and position from the huddle quickly since getting the football snapped as fast as possible helps the total offense.

SEQUENCE AT LINE OF SCRIMMAGE

Taking stance

Some coaches have players take their offensive stance on their own, while others have players assume a pre-shift stance is usually a two-point stance with hands or elbows on knees. If a team does a lot of shifting prior to the snap, it is probably better to have them go down as a unit after the shifting has been completed. Once the hand has been placed down, it cannot be lifted until the ball is snapped.

A team can run a play from a pre-shift position on first sound, and this can be an effective surprise element.

Rhythmic versus non-rhythmic cadence

The sequence of sounds uttered by the QB can be either rhythmic or non-rhythmic. Proponents of a rhythmic sequence feel that offensive personnel can anticipate the snap count and get off more uniformly and quickly. Some coaches will even have the centre delay the snap slightly to allow the offense to get an additional edge. Other coaches feel that a non-rhythmic cadence gives the edge to the offense. Through voice inflections and varied spacing of snap counts, the QB can get the defense off balance and over extended when the ball is actually snapped.

Sounds

Various series of sounds are used. Some examples are: 1) "Down, set, hut, hut...",2) "Set, go. go...",3) "Down, red 34, Set, hike, hike...." A touch snap signal can be used occasionally. This is a non-verbal signal with the football being snapped when the QB exerts pressure on the center's crotch.

Automatics

A very common system for changing plays at the line of scrimmage is through the use of a "live" colour. A team's normal cadence might be "Down, (a colour), (a number), hike, hike." Certain colours will be designated as "live" colours for a particular game. When the QB calls out one of these colours after

"Down," all players know that the play is changed to the number that follows. For example, if the "live" colours for a game are white and black and the call at the line of scrimmage is "Down, black, 37, hike," the players know that the play called in the huddle is changed to 37.

Motion

It is the QB's responsibility to coordinate the length of motion with the snap. This can be done in one of two ways. Motion can begin on a certain sound prior to the snap or with a foot signal from the QB. The QB lifts his heel in the direction of the back that is to go in motion.

ELEMENTS OF A SUCCESSFUL OFFENSE

The coaching staff

On the first chapter of this book the personal qualities and attitudes of a successful coach were discussed. Certainly a successful offense begins here.

The coaching staff must be flexible. The offense must suit the personnel. When personnel changes the offense might have to change. It is impossible to run an I-formation without a hard nosed fullback and a rugged, talented tailback. A split-T offense requires explosive linemen and backs. If a coach doesn't have a gifted passer and talented receivers, it would be foolish to run a pro attack.

Successful coaches all have a desire to learn. The coach who runs the offense he ran in college because he has never taken the time to learn anything else will soon become obsolete. Knowledge in itself is not enough, however. A coach must be able to communicate that knowledge. Good coaches must be effective teachers.

Finally, the successful coach must be able to motivate his players to perform to their maximum. Each coach will develop techniques that are consistent with his personality, but without enthusiasm toward his profession and his players, it is unlikely that any coach will successfully motivate athletes to maximum performance.

Stress the fundamentals

A coaching staff must have an excellent grasp of the basic fundamentals of offensive football and the ability to teach them to their personnel. Many coaches have noted that the fundamentals offensive football often deteriorate during the course of the season. If a coach isn't careful, he may find himself with twice as many offensive plays in late October but without the skills needed to execute them. A coach must never neglect the ABCs of the game. Some time in *every* practice must be spent exclusively on fundamentals.

Team strength

Teams that have established winning traditions continually work on strength development. It should be stressed during the season as well as in the off-season. Studies have shown that there can be considerable strength loss from the beginning to the end of the end of the season. It is now realized that strength is an absolutely essential aspect of speed. Many of the most successful teams have what are called "strength coaches".

Consistency—don't beat yourself

A team cannot sustain a consistent attack if it has an excessive number of fumbles, interceptions, penalties, and broken plays. This is especially true in a ball control type offense. It is tempting to overcoach. Many young coaches are so eager to get all the offense in by the first game that they neglect the fundamentals in order to do so. This is a big mistake. It is much better to run five plays well than to run ten in a semi-confident manner. An occasional "trick" play for a key ball game is not necessarily bad, but a successful coach knows that he doesn't win consistently with them.

Understand and evaluate defenses

A successful offensive coach must spend as much time, if not more, digging into the various aspects of defense. Modern defenses are sophisticated. There are so many defenses that a team can run and so many variations from these defenses at the line of scrimmage and in the secondary that a great deal of time must be spent understanding them. It would be a good exercise for a coach and a student of football to diagram all the basic football defenses against various formations and list the basic concerns, weaknesses, and strengths of each.

Know each opponent

The successful offensive coach must know more than just what defense an opponent runs. He must make use of every legitimate means at his disposal to learn everything he can about each opponent. Films, scouting reports, and other coaches are three obvious sources of information. File information from previous years. Organization here is essential. A coach should be able to immediately locate in his file all information on an opponent from the previous year.

Scout yourself—know your tendencies

Some coaches receive a lot of sophisticated information

on their opponents but fail to analyse their own tendencies. The coach who is aware of the scouting information that others are recording on him is better able to anticipate what opposing coaches might do in given situations.

Key for the big games

There are certain games on a schedule that a coach realizes are must games. Point for these games. A team cannot get "sky-high" for every game. A coach cannot be dishonest with his team. They know if they are obviously better. The coach who misleads his team about how tough an opponent is, will not be believed the next time. The wise coach will look at the entire schedule before the season starts and begin to formulate a plan of how to approach each game with the players in order to get a maximum effort.

Defense dictates offense

If a team's defense gave up an average of five points a game the previous season and all personnel are coming back, this will have a bearing on offensive philosophy. If the defense allows the offense to begin most drives at midfield it gives the offense much more flexibility than if it is constantly beginning drives deep in its own territory. Before the season begins the offensive coaches must realistically look at the defense, attempt to project its strengths and weaknesses, and consider this when determining offensive philosophy.

Player evaluation

Each offensive player should receive objective feedback on his performance. Some teams with large coaching staffs have elaborate grading schemes. Other coaches will make a few comments at Monday afternoon's practice. Criticism must be constructive and positive aspects of performance should be noted as well.

Simple blocking patterns

Blocking systems are the subject. The key to consistency in offensive football is to minimize breakdowns at the line of scrimmage. A coaching staff must spend a great deal of time going through all of their plays against every conceivable defensive alignment to make sure that blocking assignments don't break down.

Incentives and goals

Some coaches do a lot more in this area than others, and there is disagreement to the value of incentives and goals. Goals must be realistic. To go undefeated is something every coach strives for, but if the first game is lost and no other goals have been set, a coach will have a morale problem on his hands! Effective goal setting begins in the off-season. When the head coach talks with each athlete about next season, they can mutually establish goals for the player. The coach can also share his goals for the team and get feedback. Some of these might be: 1) to score when inside the 10-yard line to convert a greater percentage of third down plays and state a target percentage; 2) to convert a greater percentage of third down plays and state a target percentage; 3) to cut down on turnovers and state a target amount; 4) to improve on drives—the average position that the ball is given up (state a yard line); 5) to reduce penalties; 6) to score more per game; 7) to gain more first downs; and 8) to improve on quarterback sacks relative to number of passes thrown. In this way the athletes are made aware of areas of concern for the coaching staff.

Passing and running attack

Time must be spent on both aspects of offensive football. A team can go along for several games with a strong ground attack, but if they fail to develop their passing game, it will ultimately come back to haunt them. In the crucial game, when the quarterback has to throw the football, the ability to do so effectively will not be there. A team can put on an "aerial circus" for one or two games but, if that is their entire offense, it will not get them through an entire season.

Short-yardage offense

A team has to believe that they can score when they get inside the five yard line, and that they can convert crucial third and two situations into first downs. Time must be set aside every week to work on these situations. Certain basic plays that have solid blocking against stacked defenses must be explained and practised. An elaboration of offences for these situations.

The game plan

The earlier the coaching staff can decide on the game plan for a ball game, the better. Some decisions that should be made by Monday afternoon's practice are: 1) plays to work on (pass and run), 2) blocking scheme, and 3) personnel. Some minor adjustments can be made later in the week but major changes should be avoided.

COMPLETE AND CONSISTENT OFFENSE

On the face of it this recommendation may sound obvious. It is amazing how often coaches violate it. Many coaches tend to add plays in a rather piecemeal fashion as they go through the season. Before they know it, their offense is a strange mixture of formations and manoeuvres. A coach must be sure that he can attack all along the defensive front from every formation that he runs, and that he *actually does.* It's surprising how often coaches slip into the readily detectable trap of shifting to this formation for these plays and point of attack and to that formation to attack at this location. It is much better to run and pass from one formation all the time.

Two-minute offense

This element of the offense must be practised. Coaches must determine the most effective techniques to use in speeding up the offense and in wasting time, depending upon which is necessary. Games have been lost because a team unnecessarily scored too quickly, leaving the opposition time to come back and win. Some considerations.

6

HEADING THE BALL

Generally, it is said that the higher the standard of the game, the lower the height of ball at the time of passing. In other words, it means to play the ball low to the ground is considered to be one of the characteristic features of the modern game. This idea is uncontradictory with the head plays an important role in bringing the ball to the ground as soon as possible. Not only this, heading influence the speed of the specialist in the art of heading the ball as a defender and as an attacker, on occasions such as free kicks, corner kicks and centring of the passes, is of great value to the team. A convincing command of the ball with the head in an important skill used by the players Therefore, the ability to play the ball with head is of paramount importance. It is by no means a skill of secondary importance but a necessity, required by today's tactics.

The technique of heading is a whole body movement and fear is the most important element, which stands in the way of beginners in mastering the skill of heading. Therefore, it is difficult to teach also. It, in the initial stages, the contact with the forehead is made wrongly, which is painful to the beginners, they will be reluctant to make any further attempt.

Therefore, it is necessary to pay special attention to the fundamentals of heading.

Remarks on the Fundamentals of Heading

1. Surface of Impact; 2. Source of Power; 3. Take offs

SURFACE OF IMPACT

Playing the ball with forehead

Depending on the situation and time available to the player, any part of head can be used to strike the ball. But passing the ball with forehead is more commonly used for the advantage given below:

i. It is more suitable to the beginners. The forehead is the largest and the strongest part of the skull. It is not painful to the player. So the players can easily learn this skill.

ii. By using the largest surface, long trajectory can be achieved in passing. That itself is encouraging enough for the beginners.

iii. Because the ball is played with the central part of both the eyes, one can observe a larger area of the field before playing.

iv. The eyes are focused on the ball till the contact with the ball is made to assure perfect impact, as also the eyes can follow the ball immediately after contact with the ball.

v. When playing the ball with the forehead, the player is automatically standing in line with the ball.

Though there are advantages of playing the ball with the forehead, yet there is demand which should be emphasised again and again and that is to keep the eyes open. Because when and object approaches the eyes, reflex action tends to close them. Closing the eyes cannot be overcome completely. But an inexperienced player tends to close the eyes even before the impact is made. Such a bad habit must be overcome.

Playing the ball with the side of forehead

Fundamentally the use of forehead is stressed in training and even in a match. But for certain reasons, the use of the side of forehead cannot be ignored. As described earlier, the technique to be adopted depends on the aim and whether the player is stationary or jumping for the ball. Fundamentally, the action should involve as many joints as possible, in order to put all power in striking the ball. When a player is heading from standing position, he cannot utilize the body weight and joints intensively. Because he cannot use the kind of swing which he can order to have extra range in his movement from hip joint, instead of swinging the body back first and then to the ball, he sways his body to the side first in the preparatory phase, before forward swinging movement. This way he makes full use of the joints and adds power in his heading action. But only the experienced players can apply this type of technique. It is useful when the length is of primary consideration and not the accuracy.

SOURCE OF POWER

Coordination

A powerful heading depends coordinating the approach run, the jump with the leg and body action to time the contact with the ball. In body action, you need well-coordinated movements at the ankle, knee and hip joint. There has to be vigorous extension of these joints, which is imparted through the dead centre of the ball.

Role of legs in preparatory phase

Correct foot-work ensures that the player is in proper position, that is, squarely across the path of the ball. When heading from stationary position, if the whole body action is analysed, the player first performs downward and backward movement at the knee join, which is followed by upward and forward movement, the positioning of the feet may be parallel or staggered. Greater movement of the trunk backward and forward, is achieved by having staggered stance. It enables the players to sway the trunk and shift the body weight from the rear to the front foot. Therefore, there is more economical use of body mass. Consequently, the player can generate more momentum. In parallel position, the swinging movement is limited. As explained earlier, the experienced player sways his body to the side in order to have still more powerful swinging movement of the trunk.

Timing

Timing is not only important for accuracy, but for applying force on to the ball for achieving greater distance. Tall player is favoured for heading. But experiences indicate that tall body alone is not enough. The elasticity and sense of timing contribute more to the success of heading. A player should time his jump to head the ball at the peak of jump. This will guarantee maximum control and power to the header.

TAKE-OFFS

There are two ways of making jump, from standing position, and jump after short approach run. Actual situation usually determines which of these two methods should be applied. For example, if two players are standing close to each other, and one behind the other, the player standing behind has no option but to jump from stationary position. But the player in front, may have approach run and jump if he likes so. We may have another classification of jumping, that is, double leg take-off and single leg take-off. When jumping from the standing position, generally double leg take-off is performed. But when jumping after a short approach run, single leg take-of is preferred. Single leg take-off is clearly superior, because a player with single leg take-off gains considerably more height and can make use of the momentum gathered from the approach run. Double leg jump is performed when a player is caught in a cluster of opponents. He no time and space. The proper lunging position for double leg take-off is with legs slightly bent at the ankle, knee and hip joint. The trunk is inclining forward, arms are slightly extended sideways and down ready for double arm lift. A vertical jump is executed through vigorous extension of all the joints. Strengthening of trunk and double arm lift adds to the momentum.

SUB-DIVISION OF HEADING TECHNIQUE

In broader sense, there are only two main methods of heading, that is heading to the side. The other techniques discussed in some of the books are only the variations of the same. For example, heading downward and heading for distance are only the variations of heading forward. For example, you may head the ball downward or forward from standing position and from jumping position as well. Heading backward is only the modern game no player likes to play the ball on his back without seeing the area behind him, which no means he is able to see. However, for clarification, the sub division of heading techniques is given below:

Heading in standing position
—Forward
—To the Side
—Backward

Heading While Running
—Forward
—To the Side
—Backward

Heading

Heading While Jumping
Without and with approach
Forward Backward
To the side

Diving Heading
—Froward
—To the Side

HEADING FORWARD

In the preparatory phase, the player stand on the legs slightly bent at knees. Body tends to incline forward from hip joint. Arms are held near the body and are kept forward which are bent at the elbows. The player leans backward with trunk making an arc. Knees are still bent lower and pushed forward. The ball comes into contact with forehead. Contact with the ball is made during forward trunk movement from hip. At the time of contact, the knee should straighten and a forward step can be taken. The difference between the heading for distance and heading downward is point of contact If the ball is to be sent for distance, the forehead is tilted is little upward. In case of heading downward, the head is tucked downward.

HEADING SIDEWAYS

The technique of heading a ball sideways from

standing position is the same as that of heading forward. The difference between the two lies only in the backward inclination of the body and the direction in which the trunk bends. In the first phase of the movement, the player sways his back, bending his trunk and head turning the body at the same time in the required direction. The direction in which the player wants to head determines the positioning. If he wants to send the ball to the left, then the left leg is to be kept back.

HEADING WHILE DIVING

The ball reaching a player at certain height, knee or hip height, but at a distance, may be played with head while diving. A player takes-off with one or both legs and dives towards the ball. The head is kept up so that he can observe the ball and play the ball with the forehead. The arms are used to cushion the impact of body by touching the ground first.

Heading while diving should be applied in limited situations because the danger of injury is more.

7

TACKLING

The forwards only need to succeed once in every ten moves to be successful, whereas the defenders may succeed nine times out of ten and still get blamed for one mistake. That is the reason the forwards get all publicity and are commonly known in public. This is much rewarding to them But the skills executed by the defenders are not as entertaining and spectacular as the skill of a forward player. For example, scoring a goal, dribbling etc. Defensive play is remote from the scoring objective and usually does not receive sufficient publicity and recognition to provide external motivation. Therefore, in the beginning youngsters do not express their willingness to play as a defender. But thanks to the trends in the modern game, particularly after mid seventies, when the defenders can be seen flying down the wings and to get into good forward position from where they have chances of scoring. Actually, nowadays this trend has become quite spectacular. However, the defender's first and of most responsibility is do defend his own goal, and his skills should be applied to his main function of defending. Full backs, who attack as strikers, should only be considered an extension of his behaviour: basically a marker and winner of the ball. The attackers are appreciated because of his ability to manoeuvre the ball artfully. Similarly, the wizards of tacking should also receive sufficient applause.

Tackling is not important only for the defenders but equally important for the forwards. In the modern game, the division of responsibility between the so-called attacker and defender is decreasing. Therefore, the significance of tackling by all players in increasing. In 1978 World Cup the forward players of Argentina who won World Cup were clearly at an advantageous position on most occasions in winning the ball near the opponents penalty are, almost immediately they had lost. Credit only goes to the ability of the forwards to tackle. In this context, Jack Charlton had similar experience in 1966 World Cup. He said our opponents never came near us quickly because our forwards kept tackling back and regaining the ball in the opponent's area.

The technique of tacking is not only important, but difficult and painful to learn as well. Because this technique is never executed when the player is alone but he is always confronted with an opponent who certainly has better command of the ball. Therefore, a player has to have a great sense of opportunity. The other thing which creates difficulty is the execution of this technique. It is never executed for the sake of technique. It is always linked with decision taking, and taking of those decision depend upon various tactual considerations. All these tactical considerations, of course, cannot be mentioned here, but to make it clear, one example is when a defender is faced with a attacking player who has the possession of the ball, and trying to attack a defender in order to get the ball behind him. The first tactical decision the defender makes is whether to win possession or to deny possession. This immediately is followed by other decision that is how to do it. And then only he decides about what form of tickling to the be applied. The actual execution of movement is always a question of technique. The problem of how and when to use a movement is one of the tactics. It means. Besides teaching tackling, a lot of experience to the player is given to make him proficient in this technique.

CLASSIFICATION OF THE TECHNIQUE OF TACKLING

Most of the coaches do not consider a tackle successful unless the tackler gains possession of the ball. Tackling in broader sense should not be considered a complete wash out if the tackler is successful in forcing the dribbler to make a hurried pass, kick the ball out of bounds and has slowed down the pace of this forward progress, so that defender has time to recover. Tackling begins when the defender starts his move forwards the dribbler and has forced the d dribbler to change his mind of making his initially planned move. Through the tackler has not robbed the ball. Tackling tactically has two main divisions and they are not according to the particular style used by the player but according to the intention of a player. The first is winning possession which is the aim of attackers when tackling near opponent's penalty area. The other division is denying possession, which is the primary aim of defenders near their own penalty area, though the defender also needs to win possession of the ball. The other way of classifying the tackling technique is (a) a defender trying to rob the ball from the opponent in a fight which is known as direct tackling (b) he intercepts the ball before it reaches the player for whom it was passed. This is known as indirect tackle. Actually, it is difficulty to classify the technique of tackling. Since the situation and time available at the disposal of a defender is constantly changing, the generally known techniques cannot be applied. In order cope with the situation a defender may apply individual variations. According to the position of the attacker, the defender may tackle.

INTERCEPTION

A pass, directed to the man a defender is marking, intercepted by jumping ahead of the attacker from behind. The ball can be played with head of foot. The defender is faced with no particular technical difficulty in carrying out this method of tackle. Only thing that he needs is the ability to move quickly to leap for the ball, to change the direction rapidly. Metal alertness, anticipation and fast reaction are the psychological demands. A player ought to have a better sense of timing and when and how to go forward. These are primary factors which make a movement successful.

THE BASIC TACKLE

The basic tackle is further divided into two types of tackling: (a) front block tackling (b) block tackle from side.

Front block tackling

This is the most common and effectively used method, because the player is facing the dribbler right in front of him. His already blocking the direct path of the ball to the goalline. Which are the basic requirement for successful tackling. By standing in front of the ball a player is able to cut off various frontal passing possibilities. The ball is generally blocked with the inside of the foot or sole of the fool. Blocking the ball with the inside of the foot is more effective. Body weight rests on the standing leg which is bent at the meet. The tackling foot swings backward as in kicking with inside of the foot. The tackling foot then strikes powerfully in the dead centre of the ball and tries to continue in the same direction of playing. Muscles and joints of the tackling leg are kept firm. After the ball is blocked in between the two players, the tackler still maintains a balance and keeps on pressurising against the ball. The ball in second action is dragged either over the dribbler's foot or to the side.

Block tackle from side

When a defender is trying to catch up with the opponent on running almost parallel, he tackles worth the outside of the foot from side This technique is also used with variation.

The player either tries to jump and come in front of dribbler and tries to bring his outer foot in front of the ball. He is now in the position of block tackling from front. The only difference is timing and coordination. But when the tackler is not able to do so while running to the side of the dribbler, he tries to block the ball with the inner leg by keeping the out side of the foot in front of the ball. Inner foot is more effective because a player can gain valuable time. Defender should try to go close to the ball as far as possible even to use shoulder charge. The danger in applying this technique is committing a foul (tripping) and defender most likely won't be able to move with the ball. He will only be able to prevent the attacker from making his move.

SHOULDER CHARGE

Shoulder charge is the only legal means of body contact in football. If it is not delivered correctly , the player is liable to be penalised. Before learning the execution of technique, it is essential to know that the rule clearly states that charging an opponent from behind, using the elbow and charging in a dangerous manner is illegal.

The side of the upper arm and shoulder are the only areas which can be used for shoulder charge, and the opponent must also receive charge almost in the same area. The arm is to be held close to the body. The other condition for the fair shoulder charge is that the ball must be in a playing distance or must be played immediately after charge. Charging attack is executed when the defensive player is running beside the opponent. The most suitable moment for successful charging is when the opposing player is standing on outer leg. In this case, he will not be able to balance his weight on the other leg which is off the ground Moreover, he is falling to the side of standing leg. Timing and rhythm is adjusted in such a way that the player who is charging should be on his other leg. This permits a strong push off and prevents the opponent from making a quick recovery. The most common fault is that the player tends to concentrate on the ball and ignores the player.

THE SLIDING TACKLE

This method of tackling is one of the most difficult techniques. The technique is used when the attacker has managed to get pass the defender and there is no other way out by which the attacker can be dispossessed of the ball. Keeping in view the ground condition and the style of play in some of the countries, it is applied very frequently, whereas other countries are little late in applying this technique. There are some players who apply this technique even, if there is no need. Because they are in the habit of playing to the gallery. There is a considerable risk in applying this tackle. For example, sliding tackle prevents a good coordination between the defenders, because the tackler necessarily has to fall on the ground. That means, out of defensive organisation one defender is missing. Secondly, this is risky also especially when the ground is hard and when technique is not applied correctly. At the same time sliding tackle has advantage also. First, the area of operation is increased and a player can play the ball from the unfavourable condition. Secondly, the defender creates psychological impression on the attackers.

As in this technique there is a danger of committing a foul, some of the referees often penalise the tackler for dangerous play, though the sliding tackle has been executed without infringing the rules. In sliding tackle the defender has the only chance to deflect the ball away from the attacker momentarily. The defender gets no control over the ball. So the advantage is insignificant. However, technique must be applied whenever there is absolutely no other chance of tackling for the ball or dribbler is about to take a shot in the goal. If the technique is executed correctly, the defender may minimise the disadvantage and puts the team into advantageous position.

TECHNIQUE OF SLIDING TACKLE

It is performed from behind the dribbler in a

somewhat oblique direction generally with the foot of the for side. As the tackler moves up, he pick up the momentum in a natural process of running by accelerating his speed. Last stride which ends in slide is comparatively longer one. The inner leg is used for take-off, the ball is played with the outer leg (In exceptional cases it is the reverse). The body is allowed to fall on the ground by a strong bend at the inner leg. The body should be rotated in the direction of the tackling foot. This helps in sliding comfortably on the ground. During rotation, the outer part of the shin of the tackling leg touches the ground first, followed by side of the thigh, hip and trunk. The sliding and landing actions are a continuous and gradual process. The ball is played with the outer part of the foot or the front part of the toe, with complete extension of leg at the knee and ankle joint. There are other methods of sliding tackle, one such method is known as split slide tackle. In this case, the take off is done with the inner leg. This technique is more risky. The other method is hook slide tackle. This is the technique used almost exclusively when a defender is trying desperately to catch up with the opponent but cannot get close enough to make a bent leg slide tackle. Then he has to take this chance. Takeoff for this technique is made with the outer leg and the ball is played with the inner leg. The danger with playing the ball with the inner leg is that the tackler may come in contact with an opponent before the ball is played which may be infringement of the rule.

METHODICAL HINTS FOR COACHING THE SLIDING TACKLE

The individual should have his own choice of using any kind of sliding tackling. Success often depends upon the techniques which one adapts. But to adapt a particular style a lot of time is to be spent in training. To give confidence to a player and to avoid any discomfort when tackling, a coach should provide a soft surface, such as, rain soaked surface, or an artificially soaked area. Instead of using regular football shoes, training shoes should be preferred to reduce the friction and chances of injury. In training, either track suits or long pants with padding should be used.

Besides these precautions, the following sequence in training sliding tackling should be followed:

1. Falling exercise without ball. The correct technique of falling is stressed;
2. Sliding tackling towards the dead ball without an opponent;
3. Sliding tacking latterly from behind towards the ball rolling away from the player without an opponent;
4. Sliding tackling towards an opponent, leading the ball slowly and pushing the ball ahead knowingly;
5. Sliding tackle towards an opponent who moves fast while leading the ball.

COACHING TACKLING

In the training of tackling what is most important is that if a player is coming out successfully without breaking the rules and getting injured, his technique of tackling should not be changed. The known fact of the game is that the execution of tackling technique practically cannot be separated from its tactical and psychological aspects. Fear, for example, is difficult thing to conquer a player may be technically correct, but he may approach the ball halfheartedly. Therefore, the exercises arranged for the practice should be in such a way that there is a physical contact each time. Physical aggressiveness is closely related to confidence which can be built up systematically only through a realistic approach in training.

There are two types of tacklers. One is a reckless tackling defender. And the other is one who has patience and waits for the time advantage to exploit the weakness exposed by the attackers. The second defender has far better chances of success.

Sound positioning is the base for successful tackling. Correct positioning on the field and also in front of the dribbler is still improved by balance and foot-work. Body weight is distributed on both the feet in such a way that necessary and rapid shifting, change or adjusting stances are assured. That is why the sub techniques of tackling, such as, slide stepping, skip stepping and reverse retreat stepping are practised. During stepping and reverse retreat stepping are practised. During stepping, before tackling, there is. An attempt to eliminate the advantage of dribbler. Instead of challenging immediately, he establishes the most appropriate conditions for him so that tackling is done with full strength. Even when doing so, a good defender tries to force the attacker to the touch-line or to one side or take him into better tackling, position. This sub-technique is known as 'shepherding: To know when to tackle and when not to, is the other important trait to be developed in training.

Many coaches like to change the partners frequently or the position of the player in the game itself is changed, so that the defender has the opportunity to study the different individuals. Screening, as explained in dribbling, is also a requirement in tackling.

The correct and methodical procedure is to be followed. When the defender masters one stage, then only the next sequence of exercises should be followed. This type of experience in tackling safeguards the players against psychological inhibitions.

9

DRIBBLING

In spite of the fact that emphasis nowadays is on employment of all possible means to speed up the game, the easiest way to beat an opponent is by passing the ball to a team-mate: in other words, using the ball to beat an opponent. On the other hand, the opposing defenders are using the system of a tight man-to man marking. Therefore, they do not mind even going in for fierce tackling. To avoid being tackled, the pass and move method is the best. But this can only be done if a colleague is in a good position to receive the ball which is not always possible. Therefore, it becomes essential for a player to dribble and beat an opponent.

Effective use of dribbling is actually the true expression of individuality. In modern days, the players, who are skilled and courageous to accept half chances, are in great demand. They can cause confusion in a well-organised defence and help their own players to settle down and to strengthen the team's spirit and morale. While dribbing, the attackers and defenders are confronted with each other fighting for the ball. The players' knowledge, experience, reaction and technical ability is put to test against the reactions, speed and strength of the opponent.

The significance of dribbling becomes clear when the attacker beats an opponent and takes a shot in the goal. By means of dribbling, he makes a safe angle for passing. Keeping all these things in view, the significance of dribbling can be realised positively and is emphasised in the process of technique training as a strongest weapon within the principle of penetration. Dribbling is an art of using some part of foot to control the ball or roll it continuously along the ground without being disturbed by the opponent.

Here a clear distinction has to be made between dribbling and running with the ball. Running with the ball is considered to be sub-technique of dribbling. There is a large difference between running freely and unchallenged with the ball opposed to running at a defender and having to evade his challenge. That means in dribbling the opponent is by all means included. It means that irrespective of the direction, the opponent has got to be defeated. However, running with the ball and dribbling are so closely related that in training both are incomplete without each other.

TECHNIQUES OF DRIBBLING

Dribbling necessarily is maneouvering the ball to your advantage which includes guiding and driving the ball, starting and stopping with ball, turning on spot and in curves changing direction and applying feints. Since the player must run round the opponent, the ability to make use of both the feet and any part of foot are essentials of the technique of dribbling. Combining these actions means that there are a lot of variations of dribbling technique. Since it is highly individualised and personalised technique, the details of each technique is not possible.

Sub techniques of dribbling

Protecting the ball the opponent

The ball from an opponent is protected by using a method known as screening the ball. Screening generally is done by three methods, by means of change of pace, when the opponent is catching up from behind he gets rid of him by stop and go method. He stops abruptly, controlling the ball with sole of the foot, opponent reacts and prepares for tackle but then dribbler again pushes the ball forward.

The second method of screening is when body swerve and change of pace is combined. That is when an opponent is close to him, he slows down considerably, he swerves his body to the reverse direction, when the opponent is committed to tackle, he again accelerates and continues forward running. The third method is when the feint is applied with legs and is combined with change of pace. While running along side the opponent, the dribbler pretends to back heel the ball by taking his leg in front of the ball, but actually accelerates immediately at top speed.

Running with the ball

In running with ball, the objective is to initiate the move, either to get away from the opponent immediately, or sometimes, to get on tactically to the opponent defender to force him to commit himself for tackle, so that the final aim of dribbling and beating past the opponent is achieved. A player must be able to control the ball constantly and in a small area: it means touching the ball on every step, meaning that one should pay attention to lead the ball with both the legs, so that the ball is led in curves, and with changed pace. Leading the ball with outer instep is most favoured method.

Feinting

Feinting perhaps is the most important pre-requisite of dribbling which is used as a means to dislodge the opponent from the balancing position in order to have a space to be used for carrying the ball through his real move. The complete details of feinting have been given in a separate chapter on feinting. Though feints and dribbling should be taught together in training, for the purpose of study both are discussed separately. Balance, coordination, timing, speed whatever are the requirements, feints are also the requirement of dribbling.

PRE-REQUISLTES OF DRIBBLING

1. Perfect ball control even during fast movement.
2. Speed, which comprises many things like, starting speed, sprinting speed, speed of movement is an important factor.
3. Ability to run in curves and around the opponent.
4. Ability to change the pace.
5. Feinting in proper movement.
6. Match in proper movement.
7. Psychological make-up.
8. Not to apply dribble very often to have an element of surprise.

BASIC PRINCIPLES OF THE TECHNIQUE OF DRIBBLING

There are certain principles which are followed, a dribbler has more chances to come out successfully. They are summarised as under.

1. Dribbling begins with feints, to provoke reaction.

Feint should be so effective that the main action of dribbling is carried out effectively.

2. Do not approach the opponent directly.
3. Watch the behaviour of opponent before dribbling.
4. Both feet should be used.
6. Ball is kept under perfect control.
7. Change of pace is the easiest method of dribbling.
8. The skill of dribbling amounts to the ability to control the ball in limited area.

COACHING THE SKILL OF DRIBBLING

In coaching dribbling, there are two important factors which are to be recognised well. This first factor is that each player has his own of progress. Some players are proficient, confident and are in full command with the ball but rarely successful in the game. Whereas the other player who looks awkward can often be successful. Reasons can only be attributed to the physical characteristics, the knowledge of the game and psychological make-up. The other factor is in progressive and systematic training the average player can become competent and quite effective in simple feints and dribble, i.e., change of pace and change of direction. Where he assumes certain reactions and used his pure speed off the mark or changes his pace and direction. But the complex type feinting and dribbling really depends on the individual's instinctive resources.

After recognising these factors, the following sequence for training for dribbling is suggested. The first thing which should be considered in coaching dribbling is to make a player confident, relaxed and perfectly balanced in the skills which are the pre-requisites of dribbling. For example, ball control and guiding and driving the ball to his will. Practices like dodging, swerving his body, shadow dribbling, feinting against imaginary opponent, but with ball are given to have enough time to get feeling for a right sequence of a particular type of dribbling. The basic principles can be pointed out here. The player is made to run through the flags arranged in a particular manner, but before that he must learn to dodge through. Ball should be played with inside and outside of the foot. It is necessary to learn to lean and sway his body to the sides and from the hips. It is known from the experiences that actual skill of dribbling is learnt against active opponent, because to know the actual response is a must for successful dribbling, which cannot be made possible by any other means. However, the opponent first offers only unnatural resistance and then the nest stage is when both the players really fight for the ball. One by one various fundamentals of dribbling can be feint of use, only stop-and-go-method to beat an opponent and so on. This way the players develop confidence and courage which are also very important pre-requisites as a psychological make-up. The best method to develop this skill in the next stage is to ask the players to retain the possession of ball as long as possible in a small area, when he employs various types of feints and dribbling of his own choice. This of realistic approach and progression in coaching helps the players to achieve the height of success.

9

FEINTING

Nowadays, when it has become essential to mark your opponent closely, it happens many a time that a player is under pressure when he is trying to gain possession of the ball or when having possession of the ball, but wants to pass, dribble or shoot in the goal. Under such circumstances, it is necessary to act differently than what he shows. This will help in putting the opponent on the wrong foot, with the purpose to create a false impression of doing one thing but suddenly doing something else. The objective is to gain time and ground for the intended play. It means that this skill is almost executed instinctively. In other words, conscious mental stimulus is not required, and actually it is this quality which makes a player imaginative and take advantage of that split second when the opponent is off balance. But if it is conscious mental stimulus it becomes merely physical speed and the chances of a defender will improve and he may be able to counter act. In the earlier chapter on classification of football techniques, a distinction was made between the movements with the ball and movements without the ball. In this connection, similar distinction can be made between feinting with the ball and feinting without the ball.

FEINTING WITHOUT BALL

Feinting without the ball has already been explained in the chapter classification of techniques without the ball'. Besides the feints used by the defensive player and goalkeeper as mentioned earlier, feints without the ball are also executed by the attackers. For example, a player swerves a part of his body or stars running in certain direction. But his real intention is well-concealed. He determines his second move before the first move. In general, the opponent is liable to respond to the first move, but when an opponent has reacted to it he executes his planned move. There are many variations of such moves according to the differences in the individual style. But the essential thing which an player should follow is that he should not move his centre of gravity too much to the side from the vertical plane of the trunk. If the body weight is shifted to much to one side, it will be extremely difficult to execute his second move, whereas, changing the direction of action as quickly as possible is the pre-requisite of a successful feint.

Running around a fixed object, running around a movable object, rounding a partner, hoping on a zig zag line with alternate leg, following the actions of a team-mate as quickly as possible are some exercises the players can do to improve the feints without ball.

Types of Techniques of Feinting in relation to the Body position of the opponent and the technique of their execution

Feints	*Technique of execution*	*Body position of the opponent*
1. Feints While receiving the ball		

a. Feints with	Ball approaching the player on ground or in (upper or in the air, player turns his body to right\left and continues the ball to the opposite side of the turn, with inside or outside of the foot. Ball in the air can be continued with chest.	Behind
b. Kicking tennis	Kick is indicated with a powerful preparatory movement, but the ball is not kicked. Foot avoids contact but the ball is received by avoiding movement.	Front
2. *Feints while Passing*		
a. Step over feint	Kicking foot is led over to wards the manner, but in last movement it moves over the ball. In the counter movement new pass in executed in another direction.	Front
b. Kicking feint	By means of powerful visual effective preparatory movement for a pass is feinted. By suddenly breaking the movement, the ball is shortly passed. Intended direction of pass may be changed.	Front
3. Feints While Dribbling		
a. Kicking feint	Player while leading the ball powerfully swings the leg for a kick 2-3 metre in front of the opponent. Kick	Front

	is not executed but defensive movement of opponent. (protective reaction) is utilized for playing round him.	
b. Feints with upper part of the Body	Performing lauging movement to one side upper part of with upper part of the body, but the ball is the body led along the opponent with outer instep of the other foot. Body is positioned between the opponent and ball.	Front
c. Stepping on the Ball	Ball is rolled and controlled, sole ball of the foot is placed on the ball, body weight still on the rear leg. Opponent continuous running, dribbler is broken away from the opponent. He can move in the other direction or he can pass the ball.	Sideways
d. Draw back feint or dragging the	Player places his foot over the ball ball with sole. and rolls it forward. Gently, when opponent moves in with extended leg in an attempt to intercept the ball. Player drags the ball back again by moving the leg from knee. Weight of the body is kept on another leg. Ball is played around the opponent.	Front

Feinting is applied according to the need and body position of the opponent. Therefore, there is a large number of variations in the execution of this technique.

BALANCE

The first and foremost requirement is to maintain good balance to get the opponent to commit himself off balance. To maintain good balance, the centre of gravity is not moved too much to the side, because the first move immediately is to be followed by the second move which otherwise will be difficult for him.

TIMING

The opponent does not react immediately to the first move, since it takes some time to react; but if a player can time his second move, when the opponent has just reacted to the first move, that split of second is the actual time when he can perform his move successfully. It means timing and the speed of the move are major requirements.

Inexperienced players have poor sense of timing. As they are mentally pre-occupied with the whole of the action and make hasty move not allowing the opponent to react. Giving too much time to an opponent to allow him to tackle again is also bad. It is essential that the movements are executed harmoniously and rhythmically. It is very important to know that feints are not executed only for the sake of feints; it is always combined with some other technical element which is demanded tactically. Therefore, both the actions are combined with great harmony. The other important factor is when to apply feint. The time for the feint depends upon the distance at which your opponent is and the pace at which both the players are running. It is easier to deceive the opponent who is moving than and opponent who is stationary. If the opponent is at the distance of more than two yards, it is advisable to carry out the feints with the upper part of the body. Because, the opponent has time to watch the whole feint in this case and react quickly. If the distance is less than two yards, the feints with legs are executed. Because, the opponent is concentrating on the ball, so the leg actions are clearly visible to him. The player who carries out the feints, must watch the movements of his opponent keenly. He has to carry out his real movement after the reaction of his opponent. If there is no effect on the opponent, it shows either he is aware of the real intention or your action has not been so effective. A player between the age of 10-14 should be taught the following feints:

1. Feints with the upper part of the body;
2. Kicking feints
3. Feints of withdrawing foot.

It will be advisable if the players are allowed to carry out the feints in a standing position first. Then some hurdles like, flags etc., and the passive but moving opponent is introduced. Players must first become proficient with these situations, and when they are confident, only then the feints of complex nature are taught. It will advisable if the individual peculiarities are considered. So the player is watched in the match using most frequently and whether he is effective or not. Keeping these things in mind, the coach can help a player to further strengthen his skill.

OFFENSIVE SKILLS

OFFENSIVE TERMINOLOGY

Fortunately, most terminology pertaining to the offensive aspects of football is fairly standardized. Yet every coach and school have some unique terms that have significance and meaning only to them. As a result, the following list cannot be completed but it does cover most of the terms that coaches use. The terms are broken down alphabetically under five categories. The abbreviations are presented in parentheses initially and used frequently thereafter. Terminology is presented now to assist the reader as he studies this part of the book.

POSITION TERMINOLOGY

Center (C)	The offensive lineman who lines up over the football and snaps it to the quarterback (QB).
Flanker (F)	An offensive halfback set over four yards outside a tight end.
Fullback (FB)	A back lined up directly behind the center and quarterback. If two backs are directly behind the C and QB, the FB is the first one.
Guard (G)	Offensive linemen lined up alongside the C.

Strong Guard (SG)	G lined up on split end or quick hitting side of the formation.
Halfback (HB)	A back lined up approximately behind the offensive tackle.
Quarterback (QB)	Back who receives the ball from the C in most formations.
Slot Back (SB)	A back who is set between a split end and the next interior lineman.
Split End (SE)	An end who is split more than four yards from his tackle.
Tackle (T)	Offensive lineman lined up next to the G.
Strong Tackle (QT)	T lined up on split end side or quick hitting side of formation.
Tailback (TB)	When three backs (QB, FB, and TB) are lined up behind the C, the deepest one is called the TB.
Tight End (TE)	An end who is split less than four yards from his tackle.
Wingback (WB)	An offensive halfback set less than four yards outside the TE.

BLOCKING TERMINOLOGY

Running plays

Angle	A block away from the hole on a man lined up in the gap.
Bounce	When a lead blocker has the man he's blocking angling away from him he "bounces" to a linebacker.

Cross — When two adjacent offensive linemen block defensive linemen that are facing them.

Cross body — Used in crossfield block when blocker throws his body by and high past the defensive man in an attempt to chop him down.

Crossfield — Blocks made by offside linemen on defensive secondary men.

DOWN SAME AS ANGLE BLOCK

Drive — Blocking a man that is straight up and taking him out of the hole.

Gap — Same as angle block.

Influence — An attempt to decoy the defensive man into thinking that something other than the intended action is going to happen.

Inside Fold — When the interior lineman blocks to the outside on a lineman and the lineman next to him "folds" behind and blocks LB.

One-on-One — Same as drive blocking.

Outside Fold — When the outside lineman blocks down on a lineman and the lineman next to him "folds" behind and blocks LB.

Post-Lead — A double-team block where the man with the defensive man on him executes a drive block and the other blocker executes an angle block.

Pulling	When an offensive lineman runs behind the line of scrimmage and turns upfield.
Reverse Shoulder	A shoulder block when the head is not put on the hole side of the play.
Scramble	When the blocker lunges forward onto his hands, brings up his feet, and assumes a crab-like position.
Trap	When a blocker (usually a guard) pulls behind the line of scrimmage and inside-out blocks a defensive lineman or penetrating LB.

Passing plays

Cut Down	This block is used on quick passes. Blockers immediately go after defensive linemen to get their hands down.
Draw	When a blocker sets up in drop back protection to influence the defense and then blocks man away from the hole.
Drop Back Protection	Protecting a spot seven yards behind the center.
Hinge Block	Technique used by an offensive lineman assigned to protect the QB's backside.
Play Action	A pass play that comes from a running fake. The blockers attempt to block like the running play.

Screen	The blockers set up in drop back protection to influence the defense and then set up a "screen" in front of receiver.

RECEIVER TERMINOLOGY

Check Swing	The running back or end check blocks first and then slides laterally to outside.
Crack Back	This block is used by wide receivers on sweeps or tosses and is executed as diagrammed.
Cross	Pass route normally executed by TE in which he runs across the formation.
Curl	A pass receiver who goes straight down field for 8-15 yards and loops inside or outside.
Delay	A pass receiver delays before running his route.
Flag	Receiver makes outside bread to end zone flag after driving 10-12 yards down field.
Flare	A back or end runs the route shown.
Flat	A back or end runs the route shown.
Flex	When a TE assumes a wide split than normal but is less than four yards from T, he is flexed.
Hitch	When a wide receiver drives a few yards off the line of scrimmage and turns sharply to the inside.

Hook — When an end drives off the line of scrimmage for 10-15 yards and turns sharply back to the inside or outside.

Out — When an end drives off the line of scrimmage for 10-15 yards and makes a 90 degree turn to the sideline.

Pop — When an end drives off the line of scrimmage and immediately looks for a pass over his inside shoulder.

Post — Receiver makes inside break for goal posts after driving 10-12 yards downfield.

Streak — When a receiver attempts to get deep for a long pass.

Swing — When an end or running back releases laterally to the sideline.

PLAY TERMINOLOGY

Running plays

Counter — When the initial backfield flow is in one direction, but the play comes back to the opposite side.

Dive — When a halfback explodes directly ahead into the line of scrimmage and receives the handoff from the QB.

Draw — When the offensive linemen and backs set up as if the play is a pass, but the QB drops back and hands the ball off to a running back on a delayed run.

Isolation	When one back leads through the hole and blocks a linebacker, followed by a second back.
Triple Option	When any one of three backs can be the ball carrier *after* the ball has been snapped. Two defensive linemen at the point of attack are generally not blocked.
Dive Option	When the QB fakes a dive and either runs with the ball or pitches to a trail back depending on the movement of the defensive end or corner.
Belly Option	When the QB rides the FB with the ball before continuing down the line of scrimmage on the option.
Counter Option	When the initial backfield flow is in one direction, but the QB comes back in the opposite direction with the option of keeping or pitching to a trail back.
Sprint Option	The QB sprints directly down the line of scrimmage with no fake to a dive back and has the option of keeping or pitching to a trail back.
Power	Generally, a play off tackle with a post-lead block inside the hole and an inside-out block by a lead back or lineman outside the hole. A lineman generally leads the ball carrier through the hole.

Reverse — Similar to a counter with flow being established in one direction, and the ball being carried in a direction opposite to its final destination.

Sneak — When the QB keeps the ball and attempts to "sneak" past the defense, or he gets behind his blocking and "goes for the first down".

Sweep — On a sweep you pull one, sometimes both guards and have a running back or QB (on pitch sweep) lead the play around the end.

Toss — A quick end run with the playside HB taking the pitch from the QB as he goes around the end on which he is initially lined up.

Trap — When the ball carrier takes the handoff and runs behind the block of a lineman who has executed a short pull and blocked the defensive lineman out of the hole.

Passing plays

Bootleg — On a play action pass when the flow of the backfield is in one direction, while the QB reverses and throws back "against the grain."

Dropback — When the QB sprints back to a spot approximately seven yards behind the center and sets up to pass.

Play Action	When there is a running play fake before the pass.
Roll Out	When the QB reverse pivots, often with a token hand fake, before setting up beyond the offensive tackle to pass.
Screen	When the offensive linemen show pass and the QB drops back encouraging the defensive linemen to rush and the linebackers to drop back before the ball is passed to an end or back with a "screen" of blockers in front of him.
Sprint Out	When the QB doesn't reverse pivot but sprints out directly to a point wider than the offensive tackle before setting up.

OFFENSIVE SKILLS

Position requirements

The requirements and skills outlined in this chapter are those of ideal players. No coach is going to find eleven men perfectly suited to play each position. Certain offensive systems require different skills at the same position. The qualifications that follow are generalizations that would be true in most offenses.

Two characteristics must mark today's offensive football player. He must be *mentally sharp* and *physically quick*. With stunting defenses, the lineman who becomes paralysed mentally when he sees movement in front of him or is just beginning to come out of his stance when the defensive man angles by him, cannot play.

Center

Size can be additional attribute for the center in that it makes it easier for the quarterback to settle in behind him. The center must be a self-confident person. The huddle, spacing, and alignment at the line of scrimmage are initiated by him. He must know the starting count and be able to bring the ball up to the quarterback with authority. Agility is important since the center has to snap the football and then perform most of the blocks expected of other linemen.

Guards

Guards are usually not as large as tackles. They are generally quicker, since in many offenses they must pull and trap. Guards must be quick enough to cut off a roving linebacker on a 5-2 read defense, but they must also be able to take a defensive tackle head on against many even defenses. They must master a variety of blocks from the pull and trap to the post-lead, fold, and wedge. However, in option football attacks the guards are often not as quick as the tackles.

Tackles

Size and strength will certainly be advantageous for tackles in most offenses and against most defenses, but it cannot be at the expense of quickness. Tackles must win their share of head-on confrontations at the line of scrimmage, but also must get to opposing linebackers, and fold block with their guards when the blocking scheme requires them to do so. In option attacks, tackles do not have to be as big as big since they rarely block a big man aligned over them.

Tight end

The tight end must be a gifted athlete. He can be

described as a tackle who must catch a forward pass. Speed is a bonus. More importantly, the tight end must be able to block and catch the football, often in crucial situations and in traffic. A tight end who can't block consistently severely hampers a running attack to his side.

Wide receivers

wide receivers must have good hands speed. They must be in excellent condition since they will have to run on every play as if they are the primary receiver. They then must hustle back to the huddle. Courage is an important factor since wide receivers must turn and jump to catch many passes, all the time knowing that they will be hit hard the instant they touch the ball.

Quarterback

The quarterback is the offensive leader. In any offense he must be a good ball handler. He must take the snap confidently from the center and mesh with his running backs. Good faking begins with the QB.

If a team passes a lot, the QB must have a strong, accurate arm and while under pressure be able to drop back quickly, get set, pick out his targets, and release accurately.

If the offense requires the quarterback to run, he must be agile. On the option play he must make quick, correct decisions and be able to turn upfield sharply without undue loss of momentum.

All quarterbacks must have above average intelligence. Ideally, the QB should know everybody's blocking assignment on every play. Height can help him see over charging linemen. He must be willing to take charge, and he must be respected by his teammates.

Running backs

The talents of running backs vary. Some rely on sheer speed; others use power combined with a solid base plus balance. Different offenses require different qualities. All running backs must have quick acceleration, and they *can't be prone to fumble.* In most offensive schemes they will have to block a moving target while running at top speed. Running backs must be rugged since they will take a lot of hard hits during the course of a ball game. In the modern game, running backs must be able to catch the football. If the offensive system has one back carrying the ball more than the others, he should be the better ball carrier. Often-times the other backs complement him by being a better blocker or pass receiver.

FUNDAMENTAL SKILLS FOR LINEMEN

Proper fundamentals are at the heart of successful offensive football. The beginning coach is tempted to spend less time on the fundamentals so that he can get into his offensive attack and elaborate blocking schemes. This is a big mistake. At the younger ages, especially, boys need work on the fundamentals, not razzle-dazzle plays.

Stance

Everything begins from a correct stance, so it must be taught from the very beginning. A skill that has been learned incorrectly and is repeated as often as stance, is very difficult to correct.

Interior linemen will assume either a three-point or a four-point stance. The three-point is the most common. On occasion, coaches will have linemen fire out from a two-point stance. This is done to surprise the defense and catch them unprepared or in the middle of a shift.

As the offensive lineman comes to the line of scrimmage, he should immediately check his spacing and set his feet in the correct position. Most coaches state that the feet should be any where from hip width to shoulder width apart. If a lineman is moving straight ahead, a narrower width would be better, but not so narrow that he loses lateral stability. If he has to pull and trap a lot, a lineman must widen the base of support. Many young lineman have far too wide a base of support. The stance should not be too staggered. A lineman must be able to step off with either foot. A toe-instep relationship should not be exceeded. Feet should be perpendicular to the line of scrimmage. This will force the knees to be in the correct position. If the feet aren't perpendicular to the line of scrimmage, it throws the knees out of line and there is no possibility for a vigorous thrust into a block. The back should be parallel to the ground, but leg length will vary this somewhat.

There should not be too much weight on the hand or hands, but this also will vary depending upon each individual's assignments. The shoulders should be level. The hand of the rear foot (in a staggered stance) is placed directly below the eyes with either the finger tips or knuckles placed on the ground. The off forearm is relaxed and resting on the thigh just above the knee.

Center exchange

Before the center leaves the huddle he must be sure of the play and the snap count. Get up to the line of scrimmage and get set quickly, since alignment begins with you. There are two techniques used in the center-quarterback exchange.

The quarter-turn snap is the most frequently used technique. The laces should be up. The left hand carries the weight and should be on the left side of the ball with the base of the thumb at the back of the laces. The right hand is placed at the top of the laces but rolled under slightly. On the snap count, the center vigorously lifts the ball. As he lifts it, he applies a quarter turn to the football and delivers it to the waiting hands of the quarterback. The center steps out as he brings the ball up. It is the quarterback's responsibility to ride his arm forward with the snap.

In the half-turn snap the laces on the right side. The right hand is spread out and on top of the ball. The top seam is visible between the middle and index fingers. The left hand is placed palm up and under the rear of the ball, which has been elevated to a height of not more than 45 degrees. On the snap count, the center executes a swift perpendicular swing with a half turn-over and places the ball into the quarterback's hands.

One-on-one (drive) block

This is the most basic block in football and some time should be spent in every practice working on it. There are two schools of though when it comes to teaching this block. Some coaches use the shoulder block exclusively. The blocking surface extends from the clavicular surface to the tip of the blocker's shoulder and includes the blocker's lower arm. In the teaching progression, start with the linemen on "all sixes" (knees, feet, hands). On command they lunge out at a dummy. The linemen then will freeze in position while coaches check to see that: 1) there is a good neck-shoulder squeeze effect, 2) the buttocks are lower and the shoulder, and 3) the back is arched and eyes are up. After this position has been checked several times, linemen lunge out at the dummy on command. Finally, the linemen assume their offensive stance and drive the sled or dummy.

The shoulder block emphasizes *horizontal thrust*, especially during the teaching phase. Direction of thrust is largely determined by the relationship of the center of gravity (the hips) to the base of support (the feet). If the hips are well out in front of the feet, there is a lot of horizontal thrust but little vertical lift. If the hips are above the feet, there is maximum vertical lift but minimal horizontal thrust.

The question every offensive line coach asks himself, either consciously or unconsciously, is which emphasis is best. Certain blocking techniques favour horizontal thrust while others favour vertical lift. Most coaches who emphasize the shoulder block communicate to their linemen the concept of lunging. This is done from the first day when they tell their offensive linemen to dig their toes into the turf, get on their hands and knees, and explode *out* at the dummy. The word "drive" is used frequently to emphasize the action. When the linemen are on the two-man or seven-man sled they are driving it horizontally as hard as they can.

Other coaches emphasize the *vertical lifting action of the forearms*. The importance of keeping the center of gravity over the base of support is stressed.

These coaches begin with the offensive linemen's feet and knees on the ground similar to the position they are in for the shoulder block. But the shoulders and head are centered above the lower legs and the hips and forearms *roll up* into the block. The words "dip and rip" are the most frequently used to illustrate the action. When linemen are on the two-man or seven-man sled they are lifting it vertically and digging their feet as hard as they can. Linemen are taught to make initial contact with the player across from them with their forearms. The blocker must be low with his feet underneath him at contact, not sprawled out behind. Horizontal thrust is sacrificed at contact in anticipation of achieving two alternate ingredients—vertical lift and sustaining potential.

A blocker must not overextend himself. Any lateral movement or a step backwards on the part of the defensive man and contact will be lost. Against an angling defense a blocker cannot overextend in this fashion. The line of thrust must be more vertical. The player must keep his feet more directly under him and adjust to any change of direction by the defensive man.

In either blocking progression you eventually want the offensive linemen to move their defensive men out of the hole. The danger of the shoulder block is that while they lunge out, agile defensive linemen will angle by them. The danger of the forearm lift technique is that explosive defensive linemen may charge and bowl them over, since they haven't generated as much momentum.

Line splits

Line splits vary considerably from team to team and offense to offense. The speed of the backs, location of the play, relative quickness of offensive and defensive linemen, defensive stunting, down and distance, and position on the field are factors that influence the amount of split between linemen.

If a team is firing the gaps, linemen will have to tighten down. If a trap play is called up the middle and the defense is lining up on the offense, splits should be increased. When throwing the football, minimum splits will give a charging defense less room to penetrate. Tight splits make the corner closer on sweep plays. As a general rule, splits will vary from 12 inches to a maximum of 42 inches.

Pulling

Certain offenses require a greater degree of pulling, but it is a skill that is good for *all* linemen to master. Pulling is a good agility drill. The stance must be virtually identical to the one taken when firing out. If possible, shift the weight back slightly without being detected. A three-point stance is better than a four-point stance for this purpose. On the snap count, the weight is shift back and slightly in the direction of the intended motion. Weight transfer is crucial. Otherwise it is impossible to move the feet in the desired direction. Once the weight has been transferred in the proper direction, it is easy to make the first step with the lead foot about six inches back and six inches in the intended direction. Coaching points are: 1) shift weight; 2) step slightly back and in the intended direction; 3) drive lead elbow into back pocket and thrust the near arm forward; 4) push off trail foot; 5) point lead foot in the desired direction; 6) elevate body gradually, don't "pop up"; 7) keep a fairly wide running stance for purposes of stability.

The playside guard should run a "half-moon" route and the far guard should run a "sickle" path. This route will let the guard clear the center-quarterback exchange zone before he dips into the backfield. The precise route that is run on any given play is very important. Movements must mesh with a blocking back, if there is one, and the ball carrier.

Trap block

the initial movement on a trap block takes the lineman on a "sickle" path. The lineman does not need to shift his weight back as much since his route is flatter to the line of scrimmage. It is important that he stays flat. The center and guards must practice their routes often so they can pass as close to each other as possible. The blocker should stay low and aim for the upfield side of the person he intends to block. In this way he can pick up a stunting linebacker or a tackle taking a flat angling route. In any case more tackles are made because the man that is being trapped slides off the block on the upfield side.

Down, gap, or angle block

This is a block in the inside area (away from the hole) using a one-on-one blocking technique. If the blocker anticipates that the assigned man will be penetrating, he may have to cut down his split. The weight is shifted in the desired direction and the first step must be with the nearest leg. Seal off the gap first and then turn upfield, if necessary, for the block.

Reach-out block

The initial step on a reach-out block should be almost like a short trap. The line of scrimmage must be sealed. The head is aimed to the outside of the defensive man.

This is a very difficult block because it requires the blocker to block a man that is lined up between him and the intended path of the ball carrier. An attempt should be made to use one-on-one blocking techniques, but if the blocker starts to lose his man, he can resort to the scramble block.

Scramble block

Opinions differ on whether this should be a basic block. Some coaches teach that it should be used only when the blocker senses that he is losing his man on a drive block. Other coaches teach it as a basic block.

When the defensive man start to slip off the block, lunge forward onto your hands and bring your feet and buttocks up quickly. Assume a crab type position and pinch the defensive man between the thigh and upper arm. Keep scrambling with him as he attempts to free himself. The blocker's arm must not encircle the defensive man's leg, or holding can be called.

Fold block

Against many defenses these are essential blocks. Timing between the two men involved must be precise and considerable time must be spent practising it. The uncovered lineman goes first and takes a route to the defensive man that does not allow penetration. Don't go to where the man is, but to where he will be. The first step should be with the foot nearest the man to be blocked. The blocker folding behind must mesh closely. He should not loop too deep but take a jab step slightly back and in the direction of the block. He then turns up to the linebacker as quickly as possible.

Cross block

The execution of the cross block is similar to the fold

block. The blocks are executed on two defensive linemen. If one lineman is uncovered, he goes first. If both are covered, the lineman farthest from the center goes first.

Post-lead block

A post-lead block is a double-team block on a defensive man. The offensive man with the defensive man on him is called the post blocker. The adjacent lineman that is assisting on the block is called the lead blocker.

The technique of the post blocker is identical to the one-on-one block. He drives straight up and through the man and attempts to immobilize his charge. The post blocker is aware of the direction from which he will receive help but should block the man as if he is blocking him alone. It is the lead blocker's responsibility to close the seam. His first step must be with the foot nearest the post blocker. It is his fault if the defensive man splits the gap between them. He must get hip to hip with the post blocker and ride the defensive man out of the hole.

Bounce block

Oftentimes a post-lead block will develop into a bounce block. Against stunting defenses this will happen frequently. The lead blocker must come down expecting the defensive man to be coming at him, but if he angles away, the blocker must immediately bounce off to the far linebacker.

Crossfield block

Any lineman who does not have a specific assignment on a play should pick the correct angle to the running lane and meet the defensive backs who may be converging for the tackle. Once the lineman meets the defensive back, some coaches will have him gather and rip right through the man with the one-on-one block. Others suggest a high cross body block thrown at the last second and followed up with an extended roll.

Influence block

In an influence block the blocker is attempting to decoy the opponent into thinking that something other than the intended action is going to happen.

Reverse shoulder block

Generally, on any block, the head should be on the side of the hole. In a reverse shoulder block it is not. An example of when the block is used is on a down block when the defensive man is charging hard across the line of scrimmage. In order to prevent penetration the head should be thrown across the hold and the reverse shoulder used.

Basic pass protection block

Without effective pass protection blocking, any passing attack is doomed before it gets off the drawing board. The single most important aspect of effective pass protection blocking is *position*. Following are some key points: 1) don't let the man get an inside route (establish an *outside* foot to crotch relationship); 2) "hit and 'git' low"; 3) wait until he comes and explode *up* and through him; 4) don't overextend; 5) recoil after every hit; 6) don't let the rusher get his hands on the blocker; 7) know where the quarterback is setting up; 8) keep or regain separation as much as possible.

Play-action pass protection block

In play-action pass protection, the play should look as

much like a running play as possible. This type of pass is most effective in running situations. In theory, the play should be blocked just like the running play from which the pass originates. This is not always possible, but the blocker should not set up in a pass protection position immediately after the ball is snapped.

Quick (cut down) block

This block is used on all quick passes. Explode out and high at the man to be blocked. When he reacts, change your body direction and block him low. Follow through on the block and get the defensive man's hands down as he attempts to extricate himself. In this way the hands will not be in the quarterback's face as he steps up in a shallow pocket.

Screen block

Every team will have at least one form of screen pass. The exact timing, distance the linemen travel laterally, and actions will vary. The screen is intended to get the defensive linemen charging at the quarterback, who is dropping back, and the linebackers moving back to their areas of pass responsibility. The quarterback will drop the ball off to a receiver who has a wall of blockers in front of him. On this block, the linemen want to create the impression that this is a typical drop back pass. They set up in pass protection, block for two seconds, and then release to their new position. The lead blockers must not block the same person, and one blocker, usually the center, will turn back and pick up a reacting lineman.

Backside protection

Some offensive lineman is generally assigned backside protection on play-action or roll-out passes. The blocker positions himself between potential rushers and the quarterback. Use the basic pass protection technique.

Draw blocking

This play usually comes from pass action. A set-up influence block is used and the man is blocked away from the point of attack. If nobody shows, the blocker continues downfield and blocks a halfback.

FUNDAMENTAL SKILLS FOR BACKS

Stance

The basic principles described in the linemen's stance apply. The exact stance will depend upon the requirements of the position in a given offense. For example, the fullback in the wishbone attack has his feet parallel since he must run to the right and left creases with equal quickness. He also has a fairly wide stance since he will be hit from the side often and hard. If a back sprints forward most of the time, he can get into a sprinter's stance with his feet hip width apart and his weight well forward. If he must move laterally most of the time, he carries little weight on his hand. Some coaches who utilize a tailback like to have him in a two-point stance. Acceleration is not appreciably slower. In fact, some research indicates that a standing start may be the fastest.

Position

The position of the backs depends on the offense. In the wishbone attack it is generally thirteen feet from the line of scrimmage to the fullback's feet and fifteen feet to the halfback's feet. There are 18 inches between the inside foot of the halfback and the near foot of the fullback.

An I-formation will generally have the tailback five yards and the fullback three and one half yards from the line of scrimmage. A wing-back's position can vary, but he is normally one yard deeper than the linemen and between one to two yards outside the end. A halfback in a winged-T is as deep as the fullback and lined up behind the offensive tackle, approximately three and one half to four yards off the line of scrimmage.

Movement

When a running back moves forward, he rolls his weight forward and vigorously extends the trail leg (if in a staggered stance). His lead or power leg is now at an ideal angle to continue the forward thrust. The arms must act in opposition to the legs. He must continue driving with the arms until the exchange zone is reached. When moving laterally a running back can utilize the same mechanics as the pulling guard (note fundamental line skills), or he can use a cross-step. In a cross-step technique, the back pivots on the foot in the direction of lateral movement while the trail foot crosses over the front and the weight shifts in the direction of movement. Most research indicates that a cross-step is faster when the distance to be covered is greater than five feet.

Ball handling

It is the quarterback's responsibility to get the ball to the ball carrier. A back cannot look for the ball. He must be watching the hole as it develops in front of him. As he nears the exchange zone, the ball carrier simply raises the near arm on the side of the quarterback and gets the inside elbow at eye level. The forearm should be parallel to the ground with the fingers spread and bent. the palm of the far arm is facing up, with the forearm about three to six inches from the body. Some coaches state that the ball should be placed firmly on the far hip of the receiver while others feel that the ball should be laid softly against the belly as if it were an egg that you don't want to break. The runner should guide the ball into place with the upper hand as his lower arm wraps around it. A firm grip is kept on the ball and the ball is not shifted around until the line of scrimmage has been well cleared.

Faking

The ball carrier must mesh with the quarterback, stay low, and drive through the assigned hole. Fakes are continued until he is five yards beyond the line of scrimmage or tackled. Faking is just as important as ball carrying.

Blocking

The most important blocks for backs to master are the one-on-one (drive) block on a moving target and the pass protection block. On the one-on-one block the back must "gather" or "coil" just before contact and strike *up* and *through* the opponent. The technique is explained and illustrated in the next chapter. The basic pass protection blocking technique is no different than for the linemen. Inside protection is established and the attacker is driven backwards.

Ball carrying

A ball carrier can't be a fumbler. He must hang onto the football. As a general rule, the football is carried away from the initial center of formation. Most hits are received from the inside. A lot of young. Inexperienced backs run laterally too much. They should move upfield as soon as possible and use lateral movement for specific reasons such as dodging, setting up blockers, or outflanking a slower opponent. Skills that ball carriers must work on are changing direction while running at top speed, lowering-the-boom with or without a roll-off, and setting up the defense for offensive blockers.

FUNDAMENTAL SKILLS FOR RECEIVERS

Stance

Receivers use either a two-point or three-point stance. With an upright stance a receiver can perceive and assess coverage a bit more effectively.

Release and routes

A tight end must work hard at getting off the line of scrimmage. A head and shoulder fake in one direction as the weight is shifted to the opposite side often will get an end by the line of scrimmage. If this doesn't work, he can try a drive block directly at a linebacker lined up on him. Before the linebacker recovers, the tight end can drive by him. If the area is really congested, a tight end may have to scramble on all fours, get under the defense's arms, return to a running stride, and get into the prescribed pass route.

Wide receivers should release at an outside angle. This opens a larger area in which to run patterns. One exception to this is when the initial position is close to the sideline. Then a wide receiver should not take as large a split.

Receivers must be consistent in their routes. In this way quarterbacks know what to expect. Quick passes normally require cuts at four yards. Sprint out passes require cuts at eight yards and drop back and play-action passes at twelve yards. Wide receivers must learn correct depths and routes. Defenders have weaknesses and these will be spotted by good receivers. Good receivers run just as hard when they're not the primary receiver.

Receiving the football

A receiver should stay in his normal running position until the last second and only then reach for the football. If he doesn't, speed is lost. After receiving the football, a receiver normally drops the lead shoulder and turns upfield. Be a runner.

It takes a certain amount of natural ability to be a receiver. The proverbial "stone hands" are more than a myth. The three "Cs" certainly are necessary ingredients. These are confidence, courage, and concentration. A receiver has to believe that the quarterback will get him the football. The quarterback has to have confidence in the receiver. They are a team and must spend hours together working on their movements. Receivers will take some of the hardest hits of anyone on a football and are often from a blind side. It goes without saying that a good receiver must watch the ball into his hands. He must focus on the ball, not the person that is about to tackle him.

There are two opinions on how to catch the football. Some coaches say that the ball is caught with the hands and then brought into the body. They argue that the hands are softer and can absorb the force more effectively. Other coaches tell receivers to catch the football with arms and body whenever possible. Leap into the air if necessary to catch it this way. In this technique the hands are under the football. The shoulders bend and form a pocket for the ball. This technique screens the defensive back more effectively, allows the body to aid in force absorption, and results in less passes being knocked loose when the defensive man's hit occurs.

FUNDAMENTAL SKILLS FOR QUARTERBACKS

Center exchange and stance

In the quarter-turn exchange, the throwing hand is placed under the center so that the hyperextended wrist of the throwing hand conforms to the curve of the center's buttocks. Bury the hand to the wrist. The middle finger should be along the crease of the buttocks with the tip at the crotch. The elbows should be bent so the quarterback can ride forward with the center's charge without having to step forward.

In the half turn-over exchange the quarterback's hands are with the thumbs side by side and the hands spread out. His hands will naturally conform to the curvature of the center's inside thighs and crotch.

Quarterback's stances vary. Some are fairly wide and staggered and some are narrow and parallel. Since a quarterback must move quickly in both directions, it is mechanically most efficient to have the feet hip width apart and parallel. If, however, a team runs a pro-type offense with a lot of drop back passing, it would be advantageous to have the throwing leg back.

Body positions vary also. Some quarterbacks are hunched over the center; others do all the bending at the knees and the back is perfectly straight and perpendicular to the ground. The knees are bent. It is impossible to move from a stiff-legged position. Much depends upon the offense, the demands placed on the quarterback, and the body build and disposition of the quarterback himself.

Movement and ball handling

The center of gravity of the quarterback must be near the point of his base to which he moves most frequently. If he drop back passes often, his weight should be back on his heels. If it is forward on the balls of his feet, it has to travel that much farther. The fastest way to get back seven yards is to begin with the weight on the heels, sit back, vigorously turn, and sprint. On a quarterback sneak, shift the center of gravity as far forward as possible. Obviously, these shifts of weight can't be so obvious that they telegraph the quarterback's intentions.

As soon as the quarterback gets the ball, he must bring it into his navel. This serves two purposes. It protects the ball from pulling guards and crossing backs and hides it more effectively from the other team. It is interesting to note that the quarter-turn exchange has the ball in a better position for passing but the half turn-over exchange is better for handing off.

The exact movements of the quarterback will depend on the offense, but in any offense the quarterback should not take big steps. The weight should be centered and under control.

Throwing the football

Any throwing motion is very complex. An excellent book on the subject, A *Matter of Style,* has been written by Joe Namath with Bob Oates. It is a fairly scholarly presentation with excellent graphics. A quote from the book will serve as a springboard for the development of a few basic principles. "The circle and the spiral are the basic forms of motion in nature. From the swarming electrons in atomic structure to the streaming galaxies of outer space, centrifugal motion is an ever-repeating pattern."

This is a poetic way of saying that all movements of the human body are rotary. Bones move around joints aided by muscular action. The end result is often straight line motion. Throwing motions vary. All a person has to do is watch pitchers in baseball to realize this. Body weight does not have to step forward much as you throw. Movement in the direction of the throw (linear motion) can aid velocity but not if it impedes hip rotation (rotary velocity). The "quick belly button", meaning a vigorous hip and trunk rotation, is the real key to ball velocity. It also keeps you away from charging linemen. The step with your lead foot is to the side to allow for this hip rotation. As step with your lead foot is to the side to allow for this hip rotation. As the arm comes up, the hips and trunk turn. This motion puts the ball behind the head and creates advantageous muscular tension (like a stretched rubber band) before the arm drives forward into the throw.

11

OFFENSIVE SYSTEMS

Offensive systems, strategies, and formations are constantly undergoing change. The successful coach is one with a basic knowledge of all current offensive systems. The coach who refuses to take advantage of innovative trends because of stubbornness or lack of understanding will not continue to be successful. The coach who stays abreast of what is happening by reading, visiting schools with a proven record, and attending clinics will not have to feel threatened when it becomes obvious that fundamental changes to offensive philosophy must be made.

It is amazing, however, how completely ignorant some coaches are of offensive systems that they did't play as an athlete or coach. This chapter will provide an historical, progressive, and logical look at the evolution of offensive systems in American football.

In 1823 during a soccer game at Rugby School an English schoolboy by the name of William W. Ellis defined all the rules of his day by picking up the soccer ball and running with it! The "handling game," as it was often called, became a controversial issue in English schools. Young gentlemen at Eton and Harrow were issued white gloves prior to each soccer match, and the penalty was severe for any young man caught with soiled gloves at the end of the contest! Other schools, however, gladly adopted this innovative idea, and rugby began to emerge. Rules of a more definitive nature were formulated in 1871.

Rugby began to take hold in the United States after the Civil War. In 1876 the Intercollegiate Football (Rugby) Association was formed. Between 1880 and 1890 a distinctly American version of the game began to emerge. A team was limited to 11 men instead of rugby's 15, the playing field was reduced from 140 by 70 yards to 110 by 53 yards, and the scrummage was replaced by a line of scrimmage. In 1882 a system of downs was established that made it impossible for a team to hold the ball almost indefinitely. Blocking, an element so essential in American football but not allowed in rugby, emerged in 1886. Tackling "below the knees" was legalized shortly after, and the forward pass was introduced in 1906.

The origin of the huddle in American football has an interesting tale behind it. A Sports News release from Allegheny College claims that it was introduced by G. Herbert McCracken in 1924 when he was coaching at Lafayette College. The following exerpt is a quote from that news release.

> McCracken had been informed that the opposing team, University of Pennsylvania, had scouted his LaFayette squad so well for the upcoming contest between the two schools that the Penn squad knew all the plays and all the signals used by McCracken's crew.
>
> With this information in mind, McCracken

> sought a remedy which would conceal LaFayette's signals (before the huddle came into practice teams called their plays at the line of scrimmage) and therefore return the fairness to the contest.
>
> That afternoon as the teams took the field, McCracken explained to the officials what they could expect to see. Then, before each LaFayette offensive down, the team went back into a huddle to call the play, using ambiguous signals on the line just to time the snap of the ball.

The point value for various methods of scoring has fluctuated through the years. As late as 1884 a safety was 1 point; a touchdown was 2. A point after touchdown was 4; and a field goal was 5! At one point the touchdown was not allowed if the point after touchdown was missed! A touchdown was increased to 6 points in 1912. Both football and rugby continued to be played in the United States into the twentieth century, but the American version of football with its more clearly defined rules and structure became much more popular. However, in recent years there appears to be a resurgence of interest in rugby. The cost is minimal, the action is constant, and play can be enjoyed beyond the high school and college years.

SINGLE-WING ATTACK

Football is these early years was a rough and rugged sport that mirrored the values most popular in American society. The only "manly" way to move the football was on the ground and yardage made by skirting around the end was even circumspect!

The formation that pitted offense against defense in classic confrontation was the so-called "single wing." Linemen were shoulder to shoulder and when the ball was snapped, the runner was not so much tackled as he was smothered under a mass of humanity.

The rules and configuration of the game conspired against passing. The forward pass became legal in 1906 but the ball was still shaped like a rugby ball, which is much fatter, and a pass had to be thrown five yards behind the line of scrimmage.

Although the single wing is not an offensive system of any major school today, the influence of single-wing principles and techniques is certainly still present. The use of wingback, double-team blocking, trap blocking, unbalanced lines, tailback run-pass, flip-flop of personnel, and much terminology (wingback, tailback, strongside guard, etc.) all have their origin in single-wing football.

It is unlikely that today's student of football will ever coach the single wing, but a brief review of it is included here because of its historical importance and influence on the modern game.

The play from the formation that embodied plain, hardnosed football with no faking or razzle-dazzle was the off-tackle play. It was basic football. The philosophy of the play was to get to the point of attack with the most men and just mow the defenders down. this base play easily develops into a sweep by having the wingback hook the end while the blocking back and fullback lead the play. An inside reverse was soon introduced with the wingback taking an inside handoff from the tailback with the inside tackle and longside guard leading. Many people felt that the inadequacy of a passing attack brought about the demise of the single wing. A revived interest in the "shotgun" formation indicates the advantages in allowing a QB to immediately spot receivers and secondary rotations.

The punt was crucial in those days since territory was hard to acquire. Teams punted regularly and waited for the other team to make a mistake, hopefully in its own territory. The single wing was and is an ideal formation from which to quick kick.

Many football coaches and fans are unaware of an interesting interlude in offensive football that became especially evident in the professional game in the mid-thirties.

The ponderous confrontations of the single wing gave way to the T-formation during World War II, but not until several teams experienced success with a wide open brand of football surprisingly similar to today. Two of these teams were the Green Bay Packers with the legendary Don Hutson and the Washington Redskins with "slinging" Sammy Baugh.

A favourite play of Green Bay was to fake a run (play action passes are not new), isolate Hutson on one defender (defenses in those days never dropped back more than three men), and let him fake the defender out of position.

It's not hard to see why Baugh threw for so many yards. This double-wing formation allowed four receiver to get into the defensive secondary quickly, making it impossible for their defenders to adequately cover the territory.

T-FORMATION

Many individuals contributed to the development of T-formation football and heated argument can follow if one credits the "wrong" person! George Halas of the Chicago Bears, Bud Wilkinson of the University of Oklahoma, Don Farout of the University of Missouri, and Jim Tatum at Maryland often receive credit. No single individual deserves more credit, however, than Chuck Shaughnessy. He was the offensive architect of that amazing game on December 8, 1940.

The T-formation was a dramatic shift from the single wing. The tailback in the single wing had to be a master of everything-power inside runner, fast outside runner, and passer. The T-formation naturally divided these responsibilities. The QB became the passer; the QB provided the insider power; the halfbacks were utilized for quick hitting dives and speed to the outside.

The single-wing attack requires hard nosed runners, effective double-team blockers, and a good blocking back; the split-T requires explosiveness one-on-one blocking, runners capable of quickly "popping" into the open areas, and deception.

Line splits are significantly increased. Three feet between linemen is not unusual. Double-team blocking is not used as frequently. Everyone in the backfield becomes a potential ball carrier. The split-T allows a team to make good use of quick, fast charging linemen and a good running quarterback.

The formation and the basic play from it are shown in Figure 11.5. The quick handoff to the diveback is the base play from this formation. The play set up after the dive threat is established is the QB option. This was and still is one of the most exciting plays in football. In essence, it allows a team to change a play after the ball has been snapped, which puts real pressure on the defense. Nobody blocks the defensive end or outside linebacker and his movement dictates whether or not the QB keep or pitches.

TIGHT-SLOT ATTACK

At the same time that the split-T offense was becoming popular, the tight-slot attack began to be used. It combines the elements of split-T football to the "at home" halfback side, while retaining many aspects of single-wing football to the slot-back side. Much of this information is taken from Vince Dooley's book, Developing A Superior Football-Control Attack.

It can readily be seen that from this formation the split-T quick handoff can be run to the left. By putting the slotback in motion, the QB option can be run. A hard nosed power series with double-team blocking at the point of attack and a lead blocking back can be run to the right.

Since the nature of blocking assignments and techniques vary depending on whether a lineman is on the slotback or halfback side of the center, teams began designating linemen as either "strong-side or "quick" side linemen. Quick-side linemen always line up on the side of the halfback, while strong-side linemen always line up on the side of the slotback. The worlds are descriptive of the qualities needed to play on that side of the center. Quick-side linemen (QG, QT, and QE) are the linemen responsible for the blocking of the split-T series. Strong-side linemen are responsible for the power series plays.

This does not mean that teams always run split-T (quick hitting) plays to the defense's right and power (double-team with lead back) plays to the defense's left. When a team wants to run with the slotback to the defense's right they "flip-flop" as they come out of the huddle.

Designating strong-side linemen minimizes the number of blocking techniques that a lineman has to learn; it also minimizes the number of plays to be learned. For example, a ST never has to block a dive or QB option.

Backfield responsibilities also become more specialized. One back (HB) is always the dive back, one back (FB) specializes in blocking and bucking into the line between the defensive ends, and the slotback is primarily a blocker. In recent times, the role of the slotback as pass receiver has received greater importance.

Several series of plays will be diagrammed from this formation. Most of the series (with minor modifications) can be run from other formations.

POWER-SWEEP SERIES

The off tackle power is the base play that was retained from the single wing to the slotback side. The play concentrates strength at the point of attack. The tight-slot attack must make this play function. The QG leads the play. The play puts five blockers at the point of attack in front of the ball carrier.

The wide power sweep becomes effective once the off tackle power has been established. As they develop, the plays look identical. When the end or corner defender crashes down to meet the block of the fullback, he is hook blocked instead, and the play sweeps outside of him.

A halfback trap also develops from the off tackle power. The FB runs at the defensive end and the HB takes two steps as if he is going to receive a pitch from the QB. The QB fakes the pitch and gives it back to the HB as the runs at the offensive center.

INSIDE BELLY SERIES

The inside belly series has the fullback running inside tackle. If he receives the football it is with a lead back as a blocker. If he does not, his movement serves to establish flow and open the HB up on a trap or counter.

OUTSIDE BELLY SERIES

The outside belly series is comprised of two plays: 1) FB off tackle and 2) option. The second builds on the first. Once the threat of the FB has been established off tackle the QB can fake this play and have a nice option play open between him and the slotback who went in motion.

WINGED-T ATTACK

Many teams put the slot in a winged position. This is done for several reasons. It enables the back to get into passing routes more easily, especially for deep patterns. This, of course, puts the strong end in a less advantageous position for passing but a better position for blocking. However, most of the TE's routes are shallow and often delayed. The post-lead block of the back and end is better from this position. The post blocker makes contact first.

Play-action passing also can be developed more

readily from the wing as opposed to the slot. The slot (wing) back began to be used less as a blocker and more as a pass receiver. For these reasons the winged position is more popular today. Offensive philosophies also changed. The isolation play in which the slotback blocked inside, usually on a linebacker, became less popular. One-on-one blocking similar to the quickside attack began to be used more.

QUICK TRAP SERIES

One additional series that also can be run from the slot or T is the quick trap series. They are the fullback trap, the counter trap, and the take trap sweep. The FB trap is a quick hitting trap play. It is especially effective against an attacking, penetrating defense.

I-FORMATION

If a team has one running back who is definitely better than the others and is gifted at "running to daylight", the I-formation may be the best formation to run. This formation places the HB behind the FB, often in a two-point stance. From here he can run in either direction with equal effectiveness.

In this formation the FB must be a good blocker and inside runner. This is what he does almost all the time. The TB must have enough speed to get to the outside, but equally as important is a knack for knowing where a hole will open up and then the ability to accelerate through it. The split-T concept of "popping" through a hole gives way to more lateral motion behind the line and then sensing when to cut upfield.

The power series is still very effective and can be run in either direction. All blockers have to sustain their blocks longer and every block is crucial since the TB can often cut back into an unexpected location.

The sprint out series is very popular from the I-formation. The QB opens to the side of the play and sprints directly at the defensive end or corner man. The FB leads the TB as the TB keeps his pitch position with the QB. Isolation plays are now run with the FB as the isolation blocker rather than the slot back. This is a basic running play of the I-formation. The linemen "drive" block, and the TB "runs to daylight." The QB should get back and give the ball to the TB early. If the defensive LB's begin keying the FB, assuming that the TB always goes in the same direction, misdirection is effective.

PRO FORMATION

As passing became a more common method of advancing the football, the pro formation was used more often. It splits an end out in one direction and uses a back as a flanker in the other. The flanker back also can be put on the same side as the split end. This is called a wide slot and can be effective when the ball is placed on a hash mark.

The theory behind the pro formation is that if the offense can isolate one defensive back on a receive of equal ability, a good QB should be able to get the ball to him, since the defensive man can only react to the wide receiver's manoeuvres.

The pro look forced teams into many defensive adjustments. The 4-3 became the most widely accepted defense since three LBs were available to help out with the pass coverage. Their role becomes absolutely essential when teams go to double coverage on the wide receivers. Offensive linemen have to spend a lot of time one pass protection blocking since this is what they are doing most of the time.

VEER

The veer and wishbone attacks became very popular in the early 1970s. They were probably the most radical departure from offenses of the day since the introduction of the split-T twenty years before. Interestingly enough, one element in them is surprisingly similar. The pure option play of the split-T series in which the defensive end or corner man is not blocked, gives the offense two plays that can be run after the snap of the ball. It is still a basic play in most offenses.

With the advent of the veer, the point of attack and ball carrier can be any one of three different spots or players after the snap of the ball. The philosophy of the veer and wishbone attacks is similar. In this triple option not only is the defensive end not blocked but usually the next man to the inside is not blocked either.

The QB has to make decisions on the "triple" instanteaneously and correctly, but the simplicity of the basic offense allows maximum time for practice on execution. In this base play, offensive ends are releasing downfield and this makes play-action passing a "fourth" continual threat of the triple action.

WISHBONE

As already stated, the concept of the wishbone is very similar to the veer. It's triple option football. In this formation, however, all four backs must be able to carry the football. Rather than having two side receivers in the initial formation, there is only a split end.

The wishbone is a consistent ball control offense. Only the fullback runs into the heart of the defense on the "triple" from this formation. In the veer, both running backs have to be able to dive and run outside for the pitch. The formation also provides a lead back in front of the pitch back.

PASSING ATTACKS

Pass defenses today are much more sophisticated than they were in the 1970s. Many more coverage are being used. It's very hard for the QB to know in advance who in the secondary will be responsible for what. Four principles will be mentioned that must be considered in any passing attack.

Run precise patterns. Receivers cannot run sloppy patterns. They must be precise and consistent if the QB hopes to connect with consistency. Secondary receivers must run their patterns just as hard as primary receivers.

Pass protection. No passing attack can be successful without pass protection. The best pass defense is the QB sack. If a team plans to throw the football, offensive linemen must spend a lot of time working on pass protection blocking.

Know pass coverages. Secondary pass coverages will be developed. The offense must know what the other team is doing. Where are their weak personnel? How can we isolate one-on-one coverage? Careful scouting of the opposition's tendencies is crucial.

Straddling the patterns. Offensive pass receivers

should not all make their final breaks at the same time. If they do, the QB can only focus on the primary receiver at the proper time. If he is covered and the QB must shift his focus to a secondary receiver, it will occur after he has made his break and the defense will be back on him again before the ball can arrive. It is easiest for the QB if the breaks are made in sequence from left to right or right to left. In this way he can shift his gaze sequentially across the field. Having the final break on a sideline, when possible, allows the QB to throw the ball out of bounds without fear of an interception or international grounding call.

12

OFFENSIVE DRILLS

If a coach has not provided an athlete with meaningful drill practice in every aspect of his responsibilities, he has no one to blame but himself when that athlete can't perform up to expectations. To just scrimmage is not a solution either. For a coach to say that the best way to learn the game is to play the game, is a cop out. Key elements of the game must be broken down and worked on individually. This is where a meaningful drill becomes so valuable. In this context a coach can isolate what an athlete is doing and make suggestions. Athletes need positive reinforcement and constructive criticism. Nothing is more frustrating than the coach who constantly berates an athlete's performance, but gives no accompanying suggestions for improvement. The drill environment is an ideal setting for this to occur.

ONE-ON-ONE BLOCK

Following is a suggested progression for teaching the one-on-one block utilizing the forearm lift technique. The progression allows you to begin the very first day with meaningful blocking technique practice regardless of whether pads are allowed. It utilizes a reverse, progressive part teaching technique. The block is divided into seven sections, A,B,C,D,F,G, and they are taught in reverse order.

By progressive part is meant that after G has been taught , F and G are taught, then E,F, and G, and so on until all the parts have been put together into a whole unit. The parts are not isolated by themselves; each new part is added immediately to the previously learned segments.

Linemen make initial contact with their foremen. During the teaching progression it appears that the forearm is being brought up illegally. Once the entire progression has been put together, it can be seen that the forearm is the final force in a series of forces that being with the lower body and culminates with a forearm lift. The letters that were utilized in the schematic, representation will precede each paragraph.

G. As stated previously, the last element in the progression is taught first. It is the *forearm lift*. This works best against a sled or hand dummies but standing dummies can be used. The player gets on both knees, body erect, and about one foot away from the dummy. On a whistle, he bring his forearm up vigorously and makes contact with it. He must stay square to the dummy and not turn. There is a tendency for players who have learned shoulder blocks to turn the head away from the striking arm and to twist the body slightly. This forearm lifting action is done with both arms.

F,G, At the second practice, add the *hip action*. The hips roll up and into the dummy as the forearm strikes. The timing must be synchronized in order to achieve maximum striking force. This is more difficult than it might appear at first. Some athletes strike with the forearm and bring the hips up almost as an afterthought, which destroys any summation of force.

Once again, this is practised with both arms. The hips, shoulders, and head must stay square to the dummy at all times.

E,F,G. The third phase, moving backward in the progression , involves *placing the leg up* alongside the dummy on the side of the striking forearm. Many players place the foot back too far or out too for to the side. Neither of these positions is correct since the lifting action must be derived from this leg. From this position the hip action and the forearm lift are combined . The same coaching tips mentioned previously must be observed.

D,E,F,G. The fourth step is the most difficult in the reverse sequence and more time must be spent here. It is possible to isolate this part, (D) and practice it by itself. The player beings part D about an arm's length away from the dummy. If he is striking the dummy with his *right* forearm, he beings on his *right* knee. On the whistle or command, he rolls *forward* over his left knee and at the same time brings his right leg directly through as he lifts vigorously with his right forearm. This takes a great deal of practice and some of the errors that players make are: 1) stepping back with the left foot rather than rolling forward over the left knee; 2) swinging the right leg out to the side in the arc rather than bringing it directly through; 3) planting the right foot too far to the side or rear thus limiting its lifting potential; and 4) twisting the body as they approach the dummy rather than staying square.

C,D,E,F,G. The fifth step beings in the three-point stance. There is real danger at this point in the progression. Many players will now fire out on the stationary dummy completely overextending themselves in the process. To discourage this, make the player actually *tough his knee to the ground* before he strikes up and into the dummy with the opposite forearm. This phase of the progression is similar to D except that it starts from the three-point stance. Most linemen have a staggered stance with the left foot slightly forward of the right foot. In this stance the linemen will immediately roll over the left knee and strike up into the dummy with the right forearm. When rolling over the right knee, it will be necessary to take a quick jab step with the right foot before commencing the action.

B,C,D,E,F, G. In the final phase players go through the sequence *after several steps have been taken*. The player moves out of this stance and when he is approximately an arm's length away from the dummy he beings the sequence described in B through G.

The whole purpose of this technique is to place the blocker's body in the optimum striking angle at the point of contact. There are two major concerns in teaching this blocking progression. The first occurs when the shift is made to live one-on-one blocking. The problem is enhanced when blocking boards are utilized. The best way to negate the effectiveness of this block is to gopher or be so low that it is impossible for a person to generate any lifting action. This, however, is not realistic in game situations when the only time that a defensive man might submarine is no the goal line. Emphasize during one-on-one drilling that the defensive man must not get so low that the blocker can pin him to the ground.

The second concern is line surge on the snap of the ball. While linemen are learning the technique, quickness on the will be reduced. There is no question that a stance that has the center of gravity well forward and allows the player to explode horizontally on the snap of the ball will get him to the opposite linemen more quickly. The offensive linemen can do little to adjust to the movement of angling defensive men making this initial surge ineffective.

Several excellent books on offensive drills are noted at the end of this chapter. A few of the more popular drills will be explained.

BLOCKING DRILLS

Board drills

The purchase of six to eight boards (10 feet long, 12 inches wide, and 2 inches thick) is a wise investment . In the stance and start (double "S") drill the boards are lined up approximately five apart and parallel with each other. The players line up at one end. A coach calls the cadence and watches each player's stance and start as he runs the length of the board.

A dummy can be placed at the blocker's end of the board and driven across the board against varying degrees of resistance on the part of the person holding the dummy. A defensive man can be positioned at the blocker's end of the board and present varying degrees of resistance.

The blockers can face each other at the center of the board and on a snap count attempt to drive their opponent off his end of the board.

Spacing rope

To teach linemen correct spacing, buy a long rope and place knots in it where the linemen should line up. The will teach the linemen correct spacing and get them up on the scrimmage. Both can be a problem in the early going.

Seven-man and two-man sleds

Every football team have at least of each. The T-bar is better than the I-bar, especially when the forearm lift technique is taught. These sleds are ideal for the one-on-one blocking drill. If forearm lift is stressed in the blocking technique, the blockers should "dip and rip" and chop their feet in place. If driving is stressed, the blockers should move the sled across the practice field.

Bull in the ring

A defensive man in a basic football position is placed in the center of a 15-foot diameter circle. blockers position themselves around the circle and number off. A coach calls out a number and that blocker moves in to block utilizing the basic blocking progression. The blockers must gather, dip and rip, and look to the tree tops. He makes one explosive hit and withdraws. The coach calls out numbers in rapid succession.

Post-lead and bounce block drill

The defensive man lines up on the center of the three offensive men. The offence decides who will post-lead. The defensive man decides which way he will angle. On the snap it becomes a post-lead or a post and bounce block. Additions can be made to drill. The other linemen can pull. A back can be added to the drill with the LB's moving on his key.

Post-lead, drive, angle, and trap block drill

All linemen line up in two lines each other with normal splits. Groups of six work together. A coach stands behind the defense and signals the blockers to drive block, post-lead right or left, angle, trap, and so forth. A coach can have only one group go at a time so he can evaluate personal and make corrections.

Pulling drill

This drill is beneficial for all linemen even if they don't pull. Have linemen line up in a long line, normal splits, and count off by three. The coach will call out "#IS down pull to the right," or "#3s down and pull to the left." The numbers called pull in the direction stated and turn up at the hole vacated by that number. The coach an have them turn up field for 5, 10, or 15 yards. Dummies can be placed up field for them to block. the coach should check on technique and quickness.

PASS PROTECTION DRILLS

Ralston and White in their excellent book, *Coaching Today's Athlete*, suggest several pass protection Drills.

Mirror drill

Players pair off or can rotate. The offensive blocker lines up in *outside foot to crotch relationship* to the man he is blocking. The defensive man can make any move he wants to get blocker out of position. Drill can progress to full speed stressing movement, balance, and position.

Tandem drill

this drill is used to teach balance and position. Blockers work in pairs. The defensive man puts his hands on the pads of the pass protector. When he is ready, the blocker sets-up and the defensive man does everything he can to make the blocker an ineffective pass protector. He can push, pull, turn, or jerk the blocker.

Line position drill

Players work in pairs two yards apart. The blocker places one foot on a yard line and faces down the line. The defensive straddles the line. In this way the drill begins with the correct outside foot to crotch relationship. On command, the defensive man runs towards the blocker and attempts to destroyed his outside foot to relationship. The blocker must keep the two-yard distance while backing up and maintaining inside position.

Shadow position drill

Players work in pairs and face each other one yard apart. The defensive man moves laterally with the offensive man shadowing him always maintaining outside foot to crotch relationship. When the defensive man moves in and strikes a blow, the blocker pops and recoils.

Four-second drill

The interior linemen (two blocking backs can be included) block an equal number of defensive men and must protect a big dummy stationed on the throwing spot with a football on top of it. The defensive men are free to do anything they want. The blockers see who can keep their man off the "QB" most frequently. The coach should have a stop watch.

BALL CARRYING DRILLS

Change direction drill

A row of five to seven players are set up ten yards apart holding hand dummies. A ball carrier runs hard at the first hand dummy and gives it a straight-arm with his right hand (ball is held in the left hand), takes cross-over steps to his left, and sprints at the second man holding a dummy. He shifts the ball to the right hand, straight -arms the second dummy with his left hand. The ball carrier continues this process through all the dummies.

Pitch-out-drill

This is an excellent drill to teach running backs to "look the ball into the hands." Number several balls with chalk on all four panels. As the running back receives pitch-outs from the QB, he must shout out the number on the panels.

"Covering the ball" drill

this is an excellent drill to reduce fumbles. When a back is being tackled or facing any type of contact, he should place his free hand over the ball without changing the position of the ball. One or two ball carriers run at a two-man sled from ten yards away. When they are within a few yards, of the sled, they cover the football with both hands, drive their inside shoulder into the padded posts, spin quickly to the outside, run for five yards with both hands on the ball, A QB also can hand the ball off to the running back a yard away from the padded post of the sled.

Punching drill

Many of the blocking drills noted for linemen are also excellent for the backs. One more is noted here. Two defenders confront an offensive back. One defender, charges and receives a block from the back. While he resets, another defender charges and is blocked. Defenders alternate charges.

PASSING DRILLS

Sideline passing drill

The end runs a short down and out route, catches the

ball, turns up field, and fights to stay while defenders attempt to knock him out of bounds.

In-bounds drill

Same set-up as in previous drill. In this drill the coach to the sideline. The receiver must catch the ball in-bounds before he steps out-of-bounds.

Concentration drill

End receives a short pass and is immediately hit by two men holding dummies. Receiver catches the ball, puts it away, and becomes a tough runner.

Basic pass route practice

All pass receivers must be able to run all the routes required of them with *precision* and *correct timing*. This can only occur if they practice routes frequently. Make sure that all receivers know all the routes, and that they run them Consistently.

COMBINATION DRILLS

C-QB exchange drill

This is an excellent drill to check the promptness of all the centers' snaps and techniques of QBs. Have three or four centers with QBs snap the ball simultaneously. Only one QB gives a starting count. The coach can check the promptness of snaps and compare the actions of the QBs as they go through the mechanics of a given play.

Inside drill

This drill utilize the offensive interior linemen from tackle to tackle and all the offensive backs. Defensively, all linemen and linebackers from the tackle to the *inside* are used. Two dummies are placed outside the offensive tackles and ball carriers must pass these before going wide. This set-up provides a realistic but limited game-like situation. Coaches can spot errors more readily, tackles can learn to recognize different defenses and stunts, and linemen can learn to make correct blocking adjustments.

Outside drill

This drill includes all offensive linemen except the guards and all offensive backs. All defensive personnel including secondary from the offensive tackle to the *outside* are included. Dummies are placed inside the offensive tackles and the backs must run outside of them. The drill has the same benefits as the inside drill, only different plays are run.

Half-line drill

this drill included a center and one half of the offensive line with all the backs. Plays to that side of the formation are run against one half of a certain defense. Individual instruction is stressed.

Skeleton pass drill

This drill serves several functions. Some of these are: 1) to help QBs and receivers recognize different alignments; 2) to teach QBs and receivers to read various coverage; and 3) to allow QBs and receivers to work on their timing under realistic circumstances. Defensive ends or linebackers should be placed over the offensive ends to make the timing realistic. Set the drill up.

One-on-one ("oklahoma") drill

This is an excellent drill for isolating one blocker against one defensive man. A ball carrier is placed at normal depth behind the blocker. Two dummies are placed six feet apart on either side of the linemen. On a snap count, the ball carrier advances to the line of scrimmage and cuts off the offensive man's block. Since only one blocker and one defender are involved , coaches can observe errors, make corrections, and assess strengths and weaknesses quite readily.

"Dummy" scrimmage

The entire offense can be against blocking dummies or the "scout" team that just moves to contact.

Full-speed contact scrimmage

Some coaches do a lot more full-speed contact scrimmaging than others. This is where most of the injuries in practice occur.

13 SPECIAL ATTACKS

HURRY-UP OFFENSE

Many football games are won or lost in the waning moments of the first or second half. Coaches need to give more than lip service to the importance of these minutes and actually devote practice time to them. The key is speed. Everything must be done quickly. There can be no wasted time getting back to or leaving the huddle. Utilize time-outs wisely. A field goal that is scored too early when additional time could have been taken off the clock may allow the opponent time to come back. Every team must have an automatic (audible) system that allows them to run plays without huddling.

Coaches and QBs must know what situations stop the clock and call plays accordingly. Five of these are:

1) Measurement,

2) First down,

3) Out-of-bounds play,

4) Penalty, and

5) Incomplete pass.

The following is a check-list for saving or wasting time on the clock. For saving the clock :

1. Hustle at all times
2. Use QB pre-planned option strategy
3. Down rolling punts quickly
4. Use pre-planned touchdown series
5. Punt out of bounds
6. Request measurements when ball is close
7. Space time-outs intelligently
8. Hustle to huddle after the tackle
9. Eliminate the huddle if possible
10. Use quick snap counts
11. Throw sideline or out-of-bounds passes

For wasting the clock:

1. Break the huddle slowly
2. Use long signal count
3. Unpile slowly after the tackle
4. Get back to the huddle slowly when on offense
5. Run wide but stay in bounds
6. Eliminate pass
7. Never call time out
8. Take the full allotted time to place the ball in play
9. Eliminate penalties which may stop the clock
10. Keep the ball within bounds

AUDIBLES

An audible is when a play is called at the line of

scrimmage. Audibles were mentioned, but since they are an essential part of a hurry-up offense and can be used for an entire game, they will be elaborated upon here. Audibles give the QB the freedom to change a call at the line of scrimmage. The QB can also indicate "check with me" in the huddle and call the play at the line of scrimmage. A series of offensive plays or even an entire game could be called without a huddle. If time must be saved on the clock or the defense is tiring, this should be done. A coach must have confidence in his QB. If the coach calls the plays the entire game, it is unlikely that the QB will call intelligent audibles in the waning moments. The offensive coaches must spend a lot of time with the quarterbacks explaining various pass coverages, defensive line stunts, and potential weaknesses.

SHORT YARDAGE AND GOAL LINE OFFENSE

Some offenses, like the Wishbone and Power I, need little or no adjustment when confronted with a short yardage or goal-line situation. Others, like a passing attack or a team with several split receives, will have to make adjustments.

More teams are going with a double tight end offense in these situations. It provides a maximum number of blockers to stop the heavy rush and at the same time allows for play action passes.

If running against a gap defense, the offense should run plays that utilize down blocking with an inside out block by a lead back. Care should be taken in pulling a lineman. If a lineman does pull be sure the adjacent lineman away from the play executes a reach block.

Cross blocking is also a possibility provided the lineman to the side of the cross block can reach out and prevent penetration by the man in his gap.

The 6-5 is a very common goal line defense. Misdirection plays are effective against it in that they can fool the MLB, whose job it is to roam free and meet any running play at the hole. The off-tackle power is still solid. Play action passes are good. One that can be especially effective is a FB flat pattern. Boot passes can also draw an overanxious secondary in the wrong direction while a dangerous receiver cuts back against their movement.

TWO ATTACKERS

The two against one combination in an open area can be thought of as a simple game of "keep away," with the object being to have X_2 keep the ball away from the defender O_1. Normally, the player with the ball has the easiest position in the drill. The defender must race from one player to another in a vain attempt to just touch the ball.

If he just touches the ball he then replaces the passer. After one minute he is also replaced. The player supporting the man the ball also has a difficult task. He must make wide runs in an are, to get from the dead space behind the defender. A few short steps to the side by the defender will force the support player either to run yet wider on the arc, or to reverse direction and run in a wide arc in the opposite direction.

In a short time all the players are tired, but most of the work has been done without the ball.

There are a series of drills that will develop team

skills and polish combinations that can be put directly into the game.

1. The hard pass. Assume that the players begin with the support player having successfully run to the side in an arc. The player with the ball, X_1, has his team-mate in sight and can deliver a hard pass to that player's feet. The pass should be hard to get beyond the reach of the defender. Thus the first combination is a hard pass to a team-mate's feet.
2. The soft pass. There will be occasions when the support player cannot get from behind the defender. Then the pass must be played into space. This pass must be a soft pass. It must be soft for two reasons. To begin with, since the support player must run onto the ball, it is more difficult to control. Timing becomes critical. With the defender changing direction, the player wants to control the pass as quickly as possible. The soft pass helps to establish this control.

The second reason is that as the support player reaches the ball he should have eye contact with his team-mate. He wants to see where his team-mate is running after the pass, and he wants to keep his team-mate in sight in the event that he needs to pass quickly back to him.

If a hard pass is delivered beyond the support player, he must turn, with his back to the passer, and chase the ball to bring it under control. It is an easy task for the defender to get between these two players and isolate the man with the ball.

Now both of these variations can be practised at once: a hard pass to feet, and a soft pass to space.

3. The through pass. There are occasions when the two attacking players are side by side as they approach the defender. Then the man with the ball can make a lead pass between the defender and the support player. This is called a "through" pass, since the ball is passed through the space between the defender and support player. Again, this pass must be delivered so that eye contact is maintained. A hard pass downfield is wrong, as explained in combination 2 above.

4. *Go alone.* The player with the ball dribbled to the defender and then made the through pass to his team-mate. Some defenders, sensing that the pass is about to be delivered, will drop to an area between the two advancing players to prevent the pass.

In such a situation, the player with the ball should be instructed to carry the ball beyond the defender and continue downfield with his team-mate continuing to run nearby for support. This can be called "going alone" or "burning" the defender. After the players have learned all the combination, then and only then, should they be allowed the "go alone" option. Otherwise, combination drills are abandoned for the chance to go one-on-with the defender. This point must be stressed.

5. *The wall pass.* The will be times when the support player can get into a position beside the defender, after having been behind the defender. This offers the opportunity to execute a wall pass. The wall pass should be a one-touch pass as described in the section on wall passing. After this combination is executed smoothly, the player with the ball can be offered the choice of initiating the wall pass or "going alone."

6. *Outside takeover.* In an open space there will be occasions when the player with the ball can carry the ball to his team-mate by dribbling. It is best that the dribbler uses his body to screen the ball from the defender, as he moved toward his support player.

As the two players approach each other, the support player will take over the control of the ball with same foot as the dribbler, so that the ball is suddenly carried in the opposite direction.

At the last second the dribbler has only to withdraw his foot and the support player can assume control of the ball. Remember that a right foot dribble is taken over by the right foot; a left foot dribble is taken over by the left foot.

After the takeover is mastered, the dribbler can be given the option to keep the ball and just let the support player run by without receiving the ball. During a game, the task of the defender is made more difficult if the takeover combination is executed and then later on it is faked. This is another "go alone" variation.

7. *Inside takeover.* In the situation described before, the defender, sensing that he might be tricked, may back away from the dribbler to be more prepared to pick up another player. This creates space between the dribbler and the defender so that the ball can be taken over on the inside rather than the outside.

   Notice that again the same foot is used on the takeover. The ball was carried on the left foot, and picked up on the takeover by the left foot. Actually, there is an advantage in this takeover, since the support player takes over the ball with his outside foot. This gives the ball automatic screening from the defender.

Again, when this combination is mastered, the dribbler has the option to keep the ball and "go alone." To review, the two-against-one combinations are as follows:

a. Hard pass to feet

b. Soft pass to space

c. Through pass

d. Wall pass

e. Outside takeover

f. Inside takeover

g. "Go alone"

When the above combinations have been mastered, practice may be conducted in the following organization.

1. *Six players-two goals.* The format is simple. There teams of two are placed in a marked area with a goal at each end. One team of two players attacks a goal defended by one player and a goalkeeper. When a goal is scored or the ball is won, the defenders carry the ball to the opposite goal and try to score. The former attackers become the defenders. There is a perpetual motion of one team attacking. One defending and one resting at the opposite end of the field.

This could be considered a form of interval

training. Also, with each attack, the teams can be instructed how to attack...i.e., wall pass, outside takeover, etc. Finally, they can be allowed to exercise any option that they want.

2. *Five players.* In a small area players Y_1 and Y_2 try to carry the ball beyond X_1 to player X_2, who is stationary and acting as a goal. If X_2 or X_1 touches the ball, it is considered to be goal. Then X_1 or X_2 passes the ball back to Y_1 or Y_2 who attack in the opposite direction. When play gets to be smooth, the stationary end men one-touch pass the ball back into play. The defenders should be replaced every minute and the attackers every minute and the attackers every three minutes.

3. *Four players- two goals.* Here, a team of two players attacks one defender and a goalkeeper. When the ball is turned over, the defenders attack the opposite goal, which the former attackers defend with one field defender and one goalkeeper.

   Four players. Two teams of two players each are placed in a grid, 20 yards by 20 yards. Several games can be played in this organization.

   a. Remaining players surround the grid and watch to critique the work of the players in the grid. The participants play 2:1 with the extra player waiting on the side. Each time the defender *touches* the ball, he is replaced by the waiting player. After a stated time, the play of attackers is critiqued and four more players are rotated into the grid.

   b. As soon as the defender wins the ball, the resting player joins him. The player who lost the ball moves off the grid to become the new resting player.

c. When the defender wins the ball, he begins to work with the supporting attacker. The attacker who lost the ball leaves the grid, and the resting player becomes the defender.

5. *Eight players.* Two teams of two can play while the rest wait. They can rotate positions every two or three minutes. Again, the attackers can be instructed on what combination to use, wall pass, takeover, etc., and then are allowed to use any option.

6. *With keepers.* If the players are available, goalkeepers can be added to defend each goal. The play remains the same.

7. *Half-field with team.* A final drill involves the whole team on half a field. Groups or two from at midfield. A goalkeeper is placed in the goalmouth, with a single defender stationed in front of him. The remaining players are placed in a corner. On signal, player X_2 passes the ball to two-player team X_8 waiting in the center circle. They attack the goal, using a combination pass, carry the ball beyond X_1 and shoot on goal. Then a rotation is made. The member of X_8 who took the shot replaces X_1. Both X_1 and X_2 move to the end of the midfield line. The remaining member of the X_8 group gets on line behind X_7. Now X_3 passes to team X_9 at center, and the drill continues.

"On signal" means that the signal is to be given by a player waiting at the center circle. The player raises his arm as a "silent" signal that the ball is to be passed to him. Or he can point left or right-where the ball is to be played into space.

When this drill is running smoothly, a sweeper can be added behind the marking defender. The sweeper would not participate in the rotation. Other variations can be introduced according to need.

To review: This is a simple exercise that involves only three players. Each has a specific task to perform. The coach should review the tasks of each player:

1. *The attacker with the ball.* If he carries the ball directly at the defender, the supporting attacker is free of a marking defender.
2. *The support player.* He must stay *open* for a pass from the ball carrier. Sudden, rapid movement is the signal for a pass.
3. *Combinations.* The two attackers have many combinations available, such as the wall pass, the through pass, an outside dribbling takeover, an inside dribbling takeover, the overlap and a forward pass.
4. *The defender.* The defender has two major roles. He must *position* himself so that the ball carrier cannot pass to his team-mate. Having done that, the defender must *press* for the ball-hunt the attacker with the ball-smother him-shut him down!

The 2:1 drill quickly wear out the best of players. If the participants are frequently rotated, the various drills will work. Otherwise, the drill will have to end shortly.

It is best if you consider these drills to be *demonstration* drills. In all the drills that follow, it is possible to reduce the ratio to 2:1 and "play out" the defender, probably by the wall pass.

A few additional words about the wall pass are appropriate at this point.

1. The wall pass can be executed at almost any place on the field. When it is done on the top of the box, it should be followed by a strong, serious threat to the goalkeeper. However, when done further downfield, it may be followed by a long pass upfield. A drill to practice this can be constructed with four players. As in a former wall-pass drill, player X_1 passes to X_2, who wall passes back to him. However, now X_1 delivers a *long* pass to X_3 more than 20-30 yards away. Then X_1 becomes the defender, and the drill is run in the opposite direction.

2. The wall-pass variation must be practised well enough that it can be delivered in the presence of a *second* defender. There are several variations that can be practised. Let us first consider the basic alignment of players. The presence of the second defender presents the following problem.

   Player X_1 dribbles forward at defender O_1. Teammate X_2 moves in to help by being available for a wall pass, but is closely marked. What to do?

   a. With practice, the one-touch wall pass may work as defender O_2 is behind the wall passer X_2. This leaves the passing lane open.

   b. The wall pass can be delivered with the outside of the foot, curving the ball out of reach of a charging defender.

c. The wall pass can be chipped *over* the head of the interfering defender.

d. The dribbler can carry the ball beyond his defender and ignore his supporting team-mate.

e. Other variations that involve the wall passer are:

In the first variation, the potential wall passer turns *blind side* to the defender O_2 and delivers a lead pass to X_1.

Now the wall passer X_2 one-touch back passes to X_1, who then delivers a through pass to X_2. X_2 turns *blind side* of the defender and races downfield.

3. This time the wall passer X_2 square passes the ball in front of X_1, who one-touch through passes the ball between the two defenders. Again, X_2 must turn blind side.

4. In final variation, X_2 draws his defender O_2 at the dribbler X_1. Suddenly, X_2 stops and turns so that he is running behind and away from the defender. Now X_1 has only to pass between his own marking defender O_1 and the ball-watching defender O_2.

As a final word, it should be obvious that the ratio of 2:1 is a fragile relationship. Either defenders arrive to destroy to destroy it, or the participants tire in trying to hold it.

This first and final tactic advantage must be quickly seen by attacking players; taking advantage of this situation must be equally quick.

THREE ATTACKERS

While the two against one drills emphasized basic team combinations such as wall passing and takeovers, the three against one drills emphasize the basic concepts of support and use of space. At the same time the previous combinations are incorporated into the drills.

THE GRID

In a marked area of 10 by 10 yards or 15 by 15 years, three players are placed in corners of the grid or square. A defender is placed in the middle. Play begins with X_1 in possession of the ball. Since he has a team-mate to the left and right, he can pass in either direction. Thus, both players without the ball are in support positions. Initially, the defender exerts about a 50 percent effort.

The drill work begins with the ball being passed in a clockwise direction. Player X_1 passes to X_2. If X_2 has the ball, he can pass back only to X_1, as his team-mate X_3 is directly behind the defender O_1. Player X_3 must move into the space of the empty corner to be able to support his team-mate X_2. This move by X_3 shows that he understands the concept of use of space.

Now the ball should be passed to X_3 to continue the ball in a clockwise direction. X_1 must move into the vacant corner if the drill is to continue. The drill should continue until all the participants can demonstrate an understanding of the concepts of support and space. The defender should be replaced frequently.

Next, the ball should be passed in a counter-clockwise direction until the participants again demonstrate sufficient proficiency in the above concepts. Finally, the players can be instructed to pass in either direction each time they receive the ball.

OPEN SPACE

The players are now ready to practice the same drill outside the grid.

1. Player X_2 has the ball and has support to his left or right. Assume that he passes to X_1. Then player X_3 must move to a position where he can support X_1 and allow him the option of passing to the left or right.

2. Assume that X_1 now passes to X_2. Player X_1 should move in the direction of his pass to give support to the pass receiver. If the defender O_1 does not move quickly to X_2, then X_1 can overlap X_2 to offer support on the far side of X_2.

This has the advantages of giving player X_2 quick support and also giving player X_3 a shorter run for support, since he can move to the position just held by X_1, rather than the longer run to the other side of X_2.

3. The players must practice this variation X_1 on the overlap and X3 replacing him. Until they move

quickly and smoothly to be in support positions for the player with the ball. Again, the defender must be replaced frequently.

FUNCTIONAL BY POSITION

The next step in the progression is to have the players drilled according to their actual positions on the right side of the field.

The fullback X_1 and forward X_2 are out by the touchline with the midfield player X_3 between them, but further in the field of play so that a triangle is formed. The defender O_1 is marking the forward, as he is the most advanced player. The drill begins by having the fullback pass the ball to the forward. (Why the fullback passes to the forward is explained under the section, "The Dutch System.")

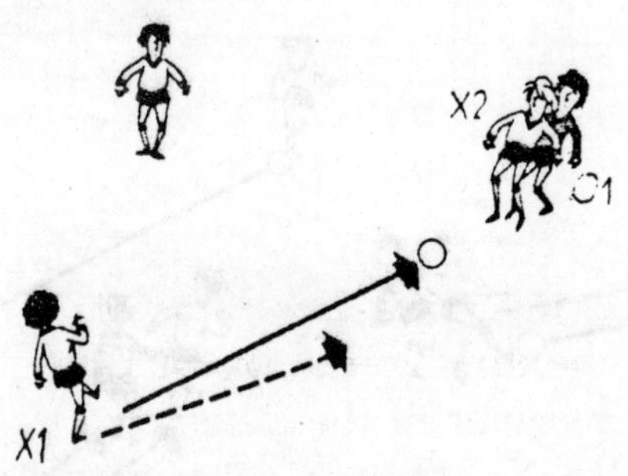

This pass must be delivered even though the forward is being marked. Both players practice playing under these conditions. In the beginning the defender is passive, so that the attacker learns to work with opposition.

The fullback moves forward following his pass.

He moves in the direction of his pass for support, and he also begins an overlap of the forward. The forward passes the ball back to the midfielder and runs in the direction of his pass. This gives support to the midfield player and at the same time draws the defender away from the touchline creating space for the overlapping fullback.

The final step is to have the midfield player deliver a lead pass to the overlapping fullback X_1. Now the midfield player runs to the near post to receive a cross from the fullback running into the corner with the ball. The wing runs to the far post and sets up on the 6-yard line.

By now you should recognize the pass combination up-back-and-through. More important, your players must recognize these pass combinations as they are developing. Then "running off the ball" is purposeful.

The players should explore alternate variations of this play. They should find and practice the variations that work for them. The following are three that should be tried. They are suggested as a starting point for further variations.

1. In the forward dribbles back toward X_3, the midfielder, while the fullback starts his overlap. The defender will have to follow to stay near the ball. Midfield player X_3 moves toward the dribbler and overtakes the ball. While the defender is briefly screened, the ball is passed to X_1, the fullback, who has been running the overlap. Now the fullback can dribble to the corner and cross to the forward, who turns and runs to the near post following the takeover by the midfield player.
2. In the second option, the forward receives the ball from the fullback, passes back to midfield, and then the forward runs to the corner before the fullback can make the overlap. The midfield player now has three options:

   a. Pass to the forward if unmarked

   b. Pass to the fullback if unmarked

   c. Carry the ball himself to the goal

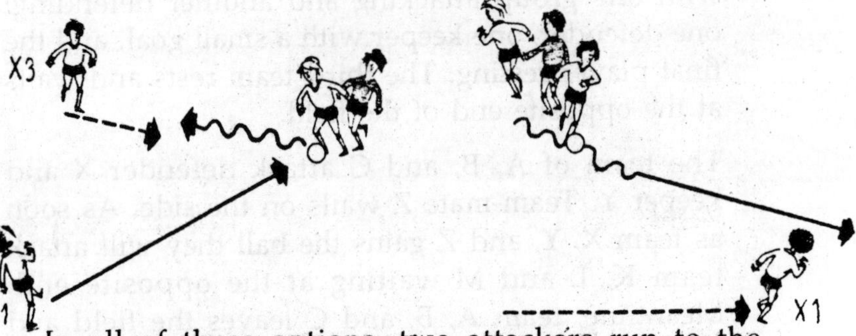

In all of these options, two attackers run to the goal-near post and far post. The drill is good for the physical conditioning of running to each post, plus the mental conditioning to see that the goal is attacked, near post and far post.

3. In the final option, the forward keeps the ball on the pass from fullback and begins to dribble away from the goal line. The fullback starts the overlap run, while the midfield starts the overlap run, while the midfield player begins a run for the corner. Then the forward passes back to the fullback. The fullback lead passes to the midfield player, who is near the touchline running toward the corner. Variations are suggested according to the position of the defender. The attackers must learn to recognize each variation and react accordingly.

PRACTICE VARIATIONS

Now that the players have executed the various combinations and understand the basic concepts, they are ready for the execution of these drills in a variety of groupings.

1. *Nine players.* Three groups of three players practice with one group attacking and another defending: one defender, one keeper with a small goal, and the final player resting. The third team rests and waits at the opposite end of the field.

   The team of A, B, and C attack defender X and keeper Y. Team-mate Z waits on the side. As soon as team X, Y, and Z gains the ball they will attack team K, L and M waiting at the opposite end. Meantime, team A, B, and C leaves the field and assumes the positions held by X, Y, and Z. This creates a perpetual three-against-one drill with one team attacking, one defending, and one resting.

Furthermore, the attacking team can be instructed on how to attack; i.e., use a through pass, a wall pass, a dribble takeover, an overlap, etc. The players must learn to recognize the various combination situations, and also learn to create such situations.

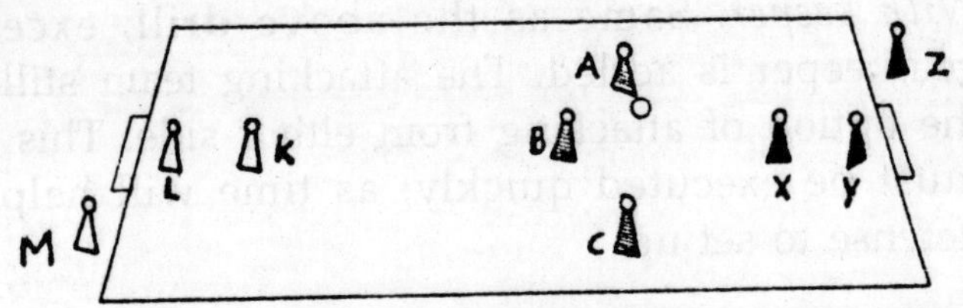

2. *Six players and two goals.* This drill can be run for only three or four minutes, as it is very fatiguing. The team with the ball uses all three players. The defending team has one field defender, one goalkeeper and the remaining player is resting. The roles are reversed when the defenders win the ball.

3. *Six players-no goalkeepers.* The Dutch buildup concept can be practised by using six players. At one end of an enclosed area, perhaps 20 by 40 yards, is a team of three players against a single defender. At the opposite end an attacking team-mate waits guarded by a single defender. When the long pass is delivered to the waiting team-mate, two players rush to his support, creating a three-against-one situation, and attack the goal.

   The ball is passed safely and under control in section A, while it is passed quickly and with risk in attacking section B. Then the direction is reversed with the buildup beginning in section B, and the rapid attack finished in section A. And so on.

4. *Four players-one goal.* Reduced to simple terms, this is three players attacking a single goal with one defender. The goal can be attacked from either side. (Diagram 10-11). This kind of drill can be run only for a short duration, as it is most intense when executed correctly.

5. *With keeper.* Same as the above drill, except a goalkeeper is added. The attacking team still has the option of attacking from either side. This drill must be executed quickly, as time will help the defense to set up.

THE BUILDUP FROM A THROW-IN

As a variation, the players can be placed on the field to execute a buildup drill ending with a quick shot on goal.

Three players are placed on the defensive half of the field. One acts as a defender, while the other two prepare to go on the attack. A third team-mate waits at the touchline with the ball. On signal, the third player throws the ball into play for safe buildup passes. These are followed by a deep pass to the forward at the other end of the field on the edge of the penalty area.

Player 1 follows his pass downfield. The near attacker, 3, follows him. Player 4 has two options:

a. He can turn and shoot. Then the player running downfield takes his place and the drill is run again. The defender should be replaced after each execution.

b. Deep player 4 can hold and screen the ball for the player coming from behind and square pass it to him for a shot on goal.

After each of these variations has been run successfully, a defender can be added to mark the deep man. In both cases, the passer alone comes from behind to support the deep man receiving the ball. Then a second player moves forward from the defensive half of the field. This creates a drill of three-against-one in a buildup leading to a three-against-one in an attack on goal. The upback-and-through is an obvious combination to be tried from this organization. A simple rotation will remove two attackers from in front of the goal, while two new players are added at the other end. A sweeper can be added to put more pressure on the attacking players.

The buildup. The man delivering the deep pass upfield must be facing the direction in which he is going to pass the ball. Avoid the situation where the passer must first control the ball, turn, and then survey the situation upfield before he can pass. The Dutch call the man facing upfield the "window" man. Consider the situation from the moment of the throw-in.

Player 1 throws to 2 who passes to 3. The chances are that 3 is facing his team-mate 2, and is not facing downfield as a window man. However, player 1 can start to run facing downfield and receive a square pass from 3 and then delivery the deadly deep pass to 4 downfield.

Here, player 1 acts as a window man and passes downfield. This is also an example of a player moving from behind the defender to open space, as was illustrated in the three-against-one drill run in the grid and with the ball being passed in a clockwise direction. Another variation, the result of player 2 back passing to 1.

Player 1 passes to 3 who has run to the empty "corner" when he initially found himself behind the defender. Now player 3 can square pass to 2 running forward. Then 2, the window man, can pass downfield. Either a square pass or a back pass will give the ball to a window man. To review: The three-against-one drills teach:

1. Support for the passer and use of space to develop this support.
2. Practice of basic combinations such as wall passing, takeovers, etc.
3. Functional practice on the playing field.
4. Development of the Dutch buildup with the window man and deep player.

THREE AGAINST TWO

In the ratio of three attackers against two defenders, the problem of maintaining numerical superiority is more complex now than in the three against one practice. It is also more game-like.

THE GRID

Three players will have a difficult time keeping possession if they short pass the ball and run into the vacant corner. While players X_1, X_2, and X_3 are interpassing, the defenders O_1 and O_2 can take turns zone defending and marking the man with the ball.

That X_2 passes to X_3. The proper movement would be to run to the vacant corner where he can get from behind the defenders. But with two defenders in the middle, that pass may be impossible. Even a return pass to X_2 is threatened by the presence of defender O_1, who is supporting O_2. The safest pass is one behind X_2.

This would have to be a soft pass that would not force X_2 to turn his back to his team-mates. Eye contact must be maintained.

A second way to move the ball is by use of the takeover. Here X_2 carries the ball in a dribble in the direction of X_3, who moves to complete the takeover. This action will draw the attention of both defenders, with one going for the ball and the other supporting.

X_3 ha carried the ball back to where X_2 started and X_1 is open for the pass, as the defender has been pulled out of position by the action of the takeover.

PLAYER MOVEMENT OFF THE BALL

What about the movement of the attackers without the ball? There are two basic concepts that must be developed:

1. Move into free space away from the man with the ball.
2. Move toward the man with the ball to support him. The following sequence will demonstrate these concepts:

There will be occasions when the two defenders try man-to-man marking instead of zone marking. This is particularly true when the attackers are working in a confined area, such as a corner of the field, by the goal line, or on the touchline.

If a defender tries to mark an attacker without the ball man-to-man, then such an attacker should try to isolate himself and the marking defender from the ball area. Now the true ratio is 2 : 1, and the two attackers should try to wall pass beyond the remaining defender. Thus, it can be said that one attacker "took away" his defender, and the two remaining attackers "walled out" the remaining defender.

Of course, if space allows, the attacker with the ball can exercise the option to go one-on-one with the remaining defender. This is an option that an attacker must be willing to take if he has the ball in the opponent's penalty area. In that area high risks must be taken.

After these concepts have been successfully demonstrated on an open field, the players can have additional pressure placed on them by practising in a confined area. Begin in a space 40 by 40 yards, then reduce the area to 30 by 30 yards, and end an area of 20 by 20 yards.

PRACTICE ORGANIZATIONS

1. *Nine players and two small goals.* Three teams of three each are placed on a small field. One team of three attacks a goal defended by two field players and one player acting as a goalkeeper. At the opposite end, the third team waits to defend. When the active defenders win the ball, they immediately move to attack the opposite goal. The former attackers rest and prepare to defend. Instruct the players to deliver the long pass across the field as well as downfield. The same concepts are demonstrated in either direction.

2. *Eight players and two keepers.* This organization allows the players to practice the buildup at the defensive half, followed by rapid attack on goal. The attacker at the far end of the field is marked by a defender and a sweeper. His movement before he receives the ball is critical. He must move to the ball.

Player X_1 moves to the touchline to receive the pass from X_2 after the buildup. He then dribbles to the endline. This initial move creates space for X_4 to come in from the other side. From the endline X_1 can long pass to X4 or short pass to X_2 coming in from behind on the same side as X_1. As a variation, forward player X_1 can run to the touchline, take the pass from X_2 and pass back to X_2. If X_2 gets inside one defender, the attack is reduced from three against two, to an attack of two against. One. Dangerous odds in front of the goal!

Many basic concepts are demonstrated in this one drill:

a. The buildup in the defensive half

b. The long penetration pass.

c. The option of a long pass or a short pass from the endline.

d. Switching. Continental play says that "you can't play without switching." Players X_1 and X_2 switch naturally in this drill.

e. For defenders, it is imperative to defend on the side, not in the middle.

f. One player stays away from the ball. Here it is X_4 coming from behind on the other side.

g. One player stays nearby for support. Here X_1 and X_2 support each other.

No drill can be exercised without a clear purpose in mind. If one drill can demonstrate many basic concepts, its usefulness is greatly increased.

3. *Six players* In a small area with two goals, three players attack two defenders. The third defender

acts as a goalkeeper. When the ball is lost or a goal is scored, the attackers fall back to defend the other goal, with two players acting as field defenders and the third as a goalkeeper.

4. *Six players, one goal.* As a variation, the drill uses only one goal which can be attacked from either side. Since one goal is used, the turnover of the ball does not give either team a chance to rest in the transition. The play tends to be more intense than in example 3.

5. *Five players.* In this variation, one player acts as the play maker for both teams. He always works with the attacking team. Also, the ball must be touched by him when the ball changes to possession by the opposite team. This is excellent for midfielders, but it is also tiring for the middle player.

6. *Five players in two grids.* In a grid of 20 by 20 yards, five players engage in a game of "keep-away" with three against two. While the three-player team has the ball, it is confined to this grid, which is surrounded by a 30-by-30-yard grid. When the two-man team wins the ball, the two players are free to play in larger 30-by-30-yard grid. If the three-player tea wins back the ball, play is again restricted to the inner grid.

There are many variations that may be introduced into this game. The two grids can be increased or decreased in size according to the skill level of the participants. The three-man team can be restricted to one-touch passing, while the smaller team can be allowed free movement of the ball. Or, time each team to see how long each unit can control the ball.

As with any other drill or practice game, make adjustments to be sure the drill works.

7. *Full team, half field.* The players are evenly placed on lines A, B, and C. The keeper is in the goal. Play begins with the first player on line A delivering a long pass to midfield between the first player on lines B and C.

   Then player A becomes a defender while the first players from lines B and C collect the ball and move at the goal, play the ball by defender A and finish with a shot on goal.

   The shooter goes to the end of line A, the defender and remaining player rotate to the ends of lines B and C. The players attacking the goal may need structure, such as being restricted to moving by the defender by a wall pass or takeover. Also, the defender may be told to give only 50 percent pressure until the drill is going well.

8. *Full team, full field.* A three against two drill can be run with the whole team on the length of the field. Two players enter the field from one side and interpass until they reach midfield. Then a long pass is made to a center forward who is marked by a marking fullback and a sweeper. The three players mount a swift attack against the two defenders. The two attackers then leave the field and the center forward remains on the field with the two defenders. Then the same drill can be run in the opposite direction, so that the completed. When this drill is run smoothly, a defender can be added at midfield, so that the drill is one of two against one followed by three against two.

A final review of concepts to be developed in training three-man units:

1. All players must kee eye contact with the team-mate in possession of the ball.
2. A hard pass can be played to the feet of an open team-mate.
3. The ball can be played softly into space, so that eye contact can be maintained with the pass receiver. Normally, space is available behind a team-mate, away from marking opponents.
4. The takeover should be tried by two players near each other. Speed must follow the takeover.
5. Attackers should try to play out one defender-isolate him-and then wall pass to him.
6. The ballcarrier should always consider the possibility of "going alone," i.e., taking on the defender 1 : 1.
7. *Passes should be mixed long and short.* There is a tendency to have three-player teams get "stuck" in a short passing game. The trainer must be alert to see that this does not happen. The long pass can be successfully played, but only with encouragement and concentration.

Finally, practice in 3 : 2 will produce many variations and player combinations. It should not be abandoned when it is achieving success. The trainer should encourage the players to become creative and imaginative in exploring the possibilities. It is not a simple drill; it is not easily mastered.

FOUR ATTACKERS

Four against two

Four attackers against two defenders is an excellent training ratio. Some coaches consider it to be artificial because the defenders have only half the number as the attackers.

Many attack concepts and defense can be taught from this formation. There is not enough defensive pressure to cause a breakdown of technique, so the tactical aspects of the game can be demonstrated clearly and efficiently.

Initially, this drill should e taught in a 15-by-15 yard grid. The four players with the ball are stationed in each corner, and two defenders are in the middle. Each groups has two basic assignments:

On attack

1. Support the man with the ball the positioning a player to his left and right.
2. Try to deliver the long through pass to the man diagonally opposite.

On defense

1. Mark the man with the ball. Cut down his passing angles. Restrict him to short, square passes.
2. The second defender must support the marking team-mate and must also prevent the dangerous through pass.

The grid

The two support players should be encouraged to leave their corners and move closer to the player with the ball. If the four players remain in their corners, the drill tends to become too static. Also, since each side is 15 yards long, it may be necessary for the players to move closer together for good ball control. A few quick, short passes should spilt the defense so that the long pass can be made to X, in the opposite corner.

Open space

Once these basic concepts are being demonstrated, the drill should be moved to an open space. Here, the vital role of the deep man can be more clearly emphasized by having him run to a deeper position.

Once he has the ball, the two team-mates X_1 and X_3 must rush to offer support to X_4. It may be necessary for the three attackers in close position to interpass until the defensive unit is spilt. Once players O_1 and O_2 begin chasing the short passes, it becomes easier for X_2 to deliver the long pass between the two defenders.

If players X_4 is unable to get free for the long pass, it is possible that either player X_1 or X_3 will move away from the group to assume the position of the deep man. In that situation, players X_4 must move in to assume a supporting role. This change still reflects a game-like situation, since often when the long pass cannot be delivered to a player positioned downfield, it is possible to make a long pass across the field to an unmarked fullback coming from behind on the opposite side.

Practice organization variations

1. *Twelve players.* Three teams of four each are organized on an area of about the width of a field. One team of four attacks another. The defending team has two field players plus one acting goalkeeper. The fourth player waits to the side. The

third team waits at the other end of the field. When the ball is won, the defenders attack the far goal, four strong, while the former attackers replace the positions held by the defenders. The rotation continues.

2. *Eight players.* Two teams of four play each other. The team without the ball uses two field players and an acting goalkeeper. The fourth player rests on the side. When the ball changes sides, the former attackers fall back and defend the far foal with two field players and goalkeeper.
3. *Eight players and keepers.* Each defending team has two field players only, The other two rest, since regular goalkeeper have been added.
4. *Six players.* Two players act as neutral midfield players and play only with the team with the ball. The ball must be touched by at least one of the neutral players before a goal can be scored. Here team Y has the ball and attacks team O. The ball must go to X_1 or X_2 before a goal can be scored against team O. Following the goal, players X_1 and X_2 automatically become part of team O and attack team Y. The neutral players must be frequently replaced.

Dutch buildup practice

At one end of the field four players begin the attack against two defenders. At the opposite end of the field two more attackers are being marked by two defenders. Assume that X_1 passes to X_2, who passes to X_4 Player X_4 is facing downfield. He is the window man who delivers the long pass to team-mate X_5 at the other end of the field. Players X_4 and X_2 rush forward to support X_5 and X_6 downfield. We now have a four-against-two situation at the defensive end of the field turning into a four-against-two situation in front of the goal.

The four attackers must move quickly against the tow defenders and score a goal. Assuming that the goal is scored, the buildup begins with two attackers who move upfield and become the two defenders. (This teaches attackers in the game, such as the forwards, to become defensive as soon as bell is list.) Now X_5, X_6, O_4 and O_3 are on the same team against X_2 and X_4. Any two of the attackers can join the group at the other end when the long pass is delivered. To help clarify the movement, attackers can be marked with triangles and defenders with squares.

Now O_4 and X_6 join in the attack and help X_1 and X_3. Therefore, O_4 and X_6 become the defenders. The rotation continues in this fashion.

Functional training

Arrange the players on the field by position and practice variation of four against two.

Fullback X_1 passes to forward X_3, who one touch back passes to halfback X_2. Then the halfback X_2 lead passes to the overlapping fullback. Meantime, the two forwards have moved toward the goal to create space along the touchline. The drill finishes with the fullback crossing to the two forwards cutting to the goal.

Here the two forwards run a takeover ending with the lead pass to the overlapping fullback. The halfback cuts to goal.

The two attackers who cross midfield become

defenders when a goal is scored or the ball is lost. The remaining four players at that end of the field begin the buildup and finish with a long pass to the other end of the field. Two out of the four attackers who are nearest to midfield cross midfield to create a four-on-two situation in front of the goal.

An easier way to run the drill is to keep the defenders as defenders, and the attackers as attackers. However, this defeats the purpose of the drill in two ways. To begin with, it forces an uneven distribution of work, since only four out of ten players are defenders. The pressure on them on them is continuous and fatiguing. Also, one purpose of the drill is to force attackers to switch to defense instantly when the ball is lost. This is accomplished only when the drill is run as designed.

FOUR AGAINST THREE

While numerical superiority is reduced is comparison to four against two, the basic concepts are the same. However, in many aspects this is an excellent grouping for training purposes. It involves one-third of all the participants in a regulation game. It also simulates the work of four fullbacks initiating the buildup against three opponents. While ball possession is demanded through a combination of short and long passes, and good running off the ball, the defensive unit can place game-like pressure on the attackers. As such, this drill may be considered to be the heart of the Dutch system.

Players X_2 and X_3 maintain support positions to X_1, who must try to make the long pass to X_4. This long, through pass quickly places the ball in an advances position and creates a dangerous threat to the opposition. This long pass is followed by a showdown while X_4 waits for team support to arrive. Support players who are close to the player with the ball run in an *arc* to open space in order to be available for a pass. Normally, support players run in the direction of their pass.

Practice organization variations

1. In a grid without goals, play a game of keep-away four against three. The grid should be 40 by 40 yards and then reduced to 35 by 35 yards.
2. Run the dame drill in an open area. *There must be a deep man at all times.*
3. *Twelve players.* Three teams of four play in a marked area. One team of four attacks a team of three defenders and an goalkeeper. The third team rests. Then the teams rotate positions. (This drill has been describes in detail in previous sections.)
4. Goalkeepers can be added to the above variations.
5. Two teams of four play each other. The defending team uses three field players and one goalkeeper.
6. The above drill can be run with one goal. The goal may be attacked from either side.
7. *Seven players.* Two teams of three each play with one neutral midfield players. (The role of the neutral midfield player was detailed in a previous section.) The neutral players is the fourth man on either attacking team.

The buildup

The buildup can be practised in a small field with two goalkeepers.

The buildup begins at one end with players X_1, X_2, X_3 and X_4 (See Diagram 11-9). At the other end of the field, players X_5 and X_6 are marked by two defenders and a sweeper. After the long pass to X_5 and X_6, two attackers move up to support the two forwards. The four attackers try to score against the three defenders. Following a turnover of the ball, the drill is run in the opposite direction.

Variations of four-against-three drills are very popular i Zeist, especially running the drill in an open area. When the players are comfortable with the drill, the attackers are limited to three-touch and then two-touch games. Finally, the four-man teams are asked to execute the various combinations learned in the two-against-one drills. Theses combinations include the wall pass, the takeover, and the through pass.

Many Dutch coaches consider this drill to be a prime vehicle for teaching tactics and technique. Drills with less than four on a side make the execution of the long pass difficult. For this reason, four-aside drills, such as four-against-three, are preferred to three-aside drills, such as three-against-two. As a final note..... We have had a Dutch National Youth Coach visit with our local youth team while they were being trained. The team was trained in the traditional drills of wall passing, etc., and they were run with the Dutch coach not showing any concern or particular interest. But when we started a 4:3 drill variation, his interest become obvious. He watched to see that there was deep man available for the long pass. He watched for support left and right of the player with the ball. He drew an arc in the air to encourage curved runs off the ball. He called for the defenders to mark man-to-man *near the* ball, and to zone mark away from the ball.

14

THREE-MAN COMBINATIONS

Three-man passing combinations are the keystone to modern soccer. By execution, there is always a long pass which opens up the game. Also, there is back passing which gives width to the attack and creates "blind-side" runs away from the ball. Within the three-man combinations there can be found the two-man combinations-wall passing, give-and-go, etc. The variations and creativeness are limited only by the ability of the players themselves.

THE BASIC DRILL

In an area about 20 yards by 20 yards, three players are stationed, one in the center and the other two in adjacent corners. One corner player passes to the middle man and runs to the nearest open center. The middle man back passes to the third player, who delivers the ball to the diagonally opposite corner where the first player has run.

The three passes are seen as follows: Player X_1 passes to X_2 and begins his run. Player X_2 back passes to X_3, who starts running out of corner slowly. Then X_3 delivers the long pass X_1, in the diagonally opposite corner. Finally X_3 runs to his adjacent corner and receives a square pass back from X1. Now the drill can be run in the opposite direction. X_3 passes to X_2, who back passes to X1, who delivers the long pass to X3. after a short square pass from X_3 to X_1, the drill is ready to be run again.

This drill should be familiar to many coaches; it is often called "up-back-and-through." However, it is really not just another drill but a keystone to the almost infinite variations of combinations that are available to groups of three players.

Finishing

Before we examine some of the three-man combinations, let's say a few words about *finishing*. Consider the options of the right outside attacker as penetrates with the ball through the final third of the field. As moves to the edge of the penalty area and enters the 18-yard box, he has many options:

1. He can drive directly at the near post for a shot on goal.
2. If opposed, he can square pass to his left to a teammate approaching centered position.
3. He can cross the ball to the opposite side to a teammate approaching on the defender's blind side, beyond the far post.
4. He can carry the ball to the goal line, somewhere between the 6-yard spot and the edge of the penalty box. From this position he can execute an angled back pass to one or more players attacking from the central positions.

Of the four options, the last is the most versatile. The advantages are many:

a. No player is offside on pass.

b. The ball is moving *away* from the goalkeeper.

c. The ball is moved into a more central and dangerous position.

In the drills that follow, the options that were just listed must be assumed as being available to the attacking player even when all such options are not placed in a given diagram or drill. To review, an outside attacker can:

1. Attack the goal directly
2. Square in the ball on a pass
3. Cross the ball to a defender's blind side
4. Carry to the end line for a back, angle pass

These are the finish elective that available to the player with the ball. With these electives in mind, let's return to three-man combinations.

FIRST OPTION

The first option is simply placing the basic pattern on a half field. In Diagram 7-2, the drill begins with X_1 passing "up" to X_2. Then square passes out to X_3, who delivers the long through pass to X_1. He then square passes out to X_3, who carries the ball toward the goal line and centres the ball, shoots or executes any of the four options mentioned before.

A simple variation of this drill is shown in Diagram 7-3, in which the play begins with an "up" pass by X_3.

Then X_2 back passes to X_1 who through passes to X3 advancing along the touchline. Player X_3 has the same finishing electives as above. The initial pass can come from an inside or outside player; the finish is the same; the variations are the same. Initially, the through pass should be delivered on the ground, but as the players acquire skill in passing and receiving, the through pass can be delivered through the air. Then any of the passes can be given in the air.

Once the variations are running well, defenders can be introduced. First a defender can mark the middle player, so that he can check in/check out in a game-like way. Then a second defender can be placed in front of the goal. As the outside, player advances with the ball, the drill becomes 3 on 1 plus a keeper. This makes the final pass by the outside player more difficult. In addition to facing the defensive players, the attackers have the additional problem of becoming *predictable*. To reduce predictability, introduce additional variations.

SECOND OPTION

Several variations can be used by having the outside player check in/check out. Now the first pass is delivered by the middle player of the group three. Player X_2 begins the drill by passing to the outside of X_3. Player X_3 square passes to X1, who has been running straight ahead. Player X_1 now delivers a through pass to X_3, who turns blind side of the defender and runs on the delivered ball. Now X_3 has the usual finishing options:

1. Shot on goal
2. Square pass inside
3. Cross beyond far post
4. Dribble to line

As a variation of this drill, player X_2 can an overlap of X_3 when he has made the first pass. Player X_2 must for the goal following his square pass. Player X_2 receives the through pass from X_1 and makes the finishing pass/run options.

Initially, defenders can be stationed as they were earlier: marking the advanced player, X_3, and zone-defending the goalmouth. The amount of freedom that the defenders are given is relative to the ability of the attackers. The drill must be allowed to succeed; opposition must stiffen when they succeed easily. At first, we instruct the defenders to mark the man, and not go for the ball. When the drill runs very well, a third defender can be introduced. Another possibility would be for the initial organization to have two marking defenders and a final "free" man, or last man.

There are several options that X_3 can try when the ball is passed to him. Instead of square passing inside, X_3 can dribble inside. As he dribble squarely across the field, X_3 should turn suddenly and deliver a long, lead pass to his team-mate running down the touchline. Which team-mate is running down the touchline? If X_2 runs inside on the first pass, then X_1 must make the run to the touchline for the lead pass from X_3.

On the dribble-in, X_3 can run a takeover combination with X1 who dribbles the opposite way to the outside, and lead passes X_2 who has run the overlap.

Who determines which variation to use? As be seen in the variations just presented, the movement of the player making the first pass, after the pass, is the movement that controls the drill. As we stated from the very beginning of this handbook,, the movement of the player with the ball is controlled by players without the ball.

The importance of the role of the player without the ball cannot be too strongly stressed. Players must learn to *move* after they pass the ball. They may move in the same direction as the ball to offer support. They may run to a more advanced position, or they may run an overlap. But standing and watching is what spectators do, not what ballplayers do.

Additional variations

There are a few more variations that can be covered. The center player X_2 can square pass the ball to the outside. This will require X_3 to run on to the ball. While this is happening, X_2 runs on an angle to the touchline and receives a pass downfield from X_3. Now the two players switch position. With X_2 in a forward position on the touchline, player X_3 runs for the near post. As a variation, three players can approach an advanced player and run the same drill. Now the advanced player runs to the touchline, and X3 who is farthest from the goal, stays behind to act as the advanced player for the next group. See Diagram 7-8.

Player X_1 passes up to the advanced player square passes the ball to X_3. Then the advanced player turns on the blind side of the defender and runs to the touchline for the return pass from X_3. Then X_3 waits for the next group to advance. When the advanced player moves after his pass, he must then learn to turn on the blind side of the defender-the side away from the ball-and make his run.

Defenders must learn to watch their opponents.

Ball watching is a dangerous habit. Attackers can "get free' easily by turning away from the ball or blind side of the defender. As attackers learn to make the blind side turn an automatic move, the effectiveness of the defenders will be reduced to a minimum.

If the ball is square passed inside, then the advanced player runs for the far post and X_3 runs down the touchline for the through pass from X_1. Now X_2 replaces the advanced player, and the drill ends in the usual way. Also, if the middle player square passes or back passes to the same side from which he received the received the ball, that is normally a signal that a wall pass will follow.

Player X_1 passes up to X_2 who square passes back to X_1. Now X_2 runs ahead to a support position to execute the wall pass with X_1, who then passes to X_3 running down the sideline.

If too much attention is called to the progress of the ball down one side of the field, the defensive unit can be surprised by having the ball delivered to the opposite side to an overlapping fullback.

Player X_2 can square pass to the left of the fullback, or player X_1 can do this following the wall-pass combination. Since the fullback creates a fourth attacking position, and we are now concentrating on the three-man units, we will not dwell on the possibilities. It is sufficient to say that overlapping fullbacks add yet another dimension to the game. However, fullbacks will not run up on the attack unless the ball is *delivered* to them. There must be a payoff for the defender who has run the overlap.

TWIN STRIKERS

One final variation will demonstrate how the up-back-through concept works with *two* advanced players. Player X_3 passes to X_1 who square passes to X2 the other striker. Then X_2 back passes to X_3 who has moved straight forward. After X_1 and X_2 have passed the ball, they each run a crisscross pattern that carries them to the opposite goal post. This gives X_3 some options, but let us look at what happens on the crisscross runs.

If X_1 square passes and runs toward the left post, X_2 may be able to deliver a lead pass to X_1 knowing where his run will carry him. Or, X_3 can one-touch the ball in the same direction to X_1. Then X_1 can square out to X_2 who is now on the right. Then X_2 can shoot or carry the ball to the goal line as with all previous drill options. If there is good defensive pressure, player X_3 can pass to X_2 running to the outside right.

If defenders are marking X_1 and X_2, and they follow these two in crisscross, there is nothing to stop X_3 from running in for a direct shot on goal. If a defender drops off his marked attacker at the last minute, then the wall pass is "on," as the defender has created a 2v 1 situation.

Players must learn to read these variations as they appear on the field. Reducing the attack 2v 1 front of the goal gives the numerical superiority to the attackers. They must use the opportunity for the brief time that they enjoy having it. Suppose that X_3 began by passing to X_2 on the first pass? There are many possible variations-think about it!

You have seen the three-man combinations begin with up-back through passes. Then familiar combinations were added: wall passes, takeover from a dribble, overlapping, place changing, and crosses to the opposite side. The variations are almost limitless, but certain patterns begin to emerge.

1. The finish (shot on goal) electives are always the same.
2. Movement following a pass has a direct effect on the combination that develops.
3. Participants can quickly learn and recognize the various patterns.
4. Variations are available to reduce predictability.

Three-man passing combinations are the keystone of modern soccer; they can absorb all two-man combinations to present an almost infinite variety of attack patterns to defenders. Modern soccer cannot exist without three-man combination.

15

BLOCKING SYSTEMS

INTRODUCTION

The development of a blocking system that is easy to understand, but at the same time complete and adaptable, is the single most important element in offensive football. A large part of the offensive staffs time will be spent checking the blocking patterns of all plays against every defensive alignment.

Once blocking assignments have been decided, the best way of communicating them to the players must be determined. Some athletes with greater conceptual abilities will profit from a more theoretical development of the offense; others will not. Everyone learns differently. Memorization of one's position assignments by rote does not make for permanent learning; yet for certain people this is the best approach. Other athletes want to know why a particular offense was selected, the philosophy behind it, and the rationale behind every play. Coaches must be willing to provide this.

In practical terms, this means that a coaching staff should begin each season by explaining to the players why a particular offense has been chosen; and if it has been changed, the reasons for the change. When position coaches present the plays, the entire play should be presented before individual assignments are covered. This ideally can be done in a classroom setting. If the use of a classroom is not practical, it can be done on the field. A veteran offense can line up on the ball and one by one give their assignments to the rest of the team. People learn at different rates and for this reason a playbook is a valuable tool. Some athletes will know their assignments after the coach has put a play on the blackboard once, but others will need frequent review. For these athletes, a playbook that they can take home and view on their own is a valuable learning aid.

BY DEFENSE

In this system, every play in the offense is diagrammed against every defense that a team anticipates seeing. They are drawn up by one of the offensive coaches, duplicated and distributed to the team.

COUNT SYSTEM

In a typical count system the defensive men along the line of scrimmage will be given numbers. If a man is directly on the center, he is not numbered and is blocked by the center. Count systems can include secondary personnel and be numbered from the outside in. This is how blocking assignments are often determined in the popular wishbone attack.

RULE SYSTEM

Rule blocking became popular with the advent of split-T, tight slot, and winged-T attacks.

ONE-ON-ONE (SPLIT-T) BLOCKING

In this blocking scheme holes are numbered over the offensive men. The numbers assigned are immaterial as long as everyone understands them. A 27 Dive would be over left tackle. The rule for the lineman of the hole, in case the left tackle, is over, inside, outside, LB. For the first man outside the hole, his rule is over, his rule is over, outside, LB. It takes practice and communication on the part of the offensive linemen to insure that they interpret the location of defensive personnel consistently. Following are definitions to assist in interpretation. Over-if the defensive lineman's helmet would hit the offensive lineman's helmet if they moved straight ahead. Inside-if the defensive man is inside but not over the next lineman to the inside. Outside-if the defensive man is outside but not over the next lineman to the outside. If a lineman is not next to the hole man, his assignment is over, LB. cutoff.

CROSSBLOCKING

If a 27 Dive X is called, it means a *crossblock* at the point of attack. A crossblock always involves the hole man, in this case the tackle, and the man inside him, in this case the guard. The uncovered lineman goes first and they simply switch assignments. The two linemen adjacent to the crossblockers must keep the next linemen away from closing down on the hole. If there are no dangerous linemen, they get the most dangerous LB. The rules are consistent all across the line of scrimmage.

POST-LEAD WITH INSIDE-OUT BLOCKING

The fundamental idea of this blocking system is to get a double team or post-lead block on the lineman *inside* the hole and an and an inside-out block by a pulling lineman or back on the lineman *outside* the hole. The first lineman outside the hole will go *across* to LB. and the next lineman to the outside or wingback will block the near LB. The rules have two parts for the offensive player at the hole, the *principle* rule and the secondary rule. His principle rule is lead (Block), and his secondary rule is, if nobody to lead on, pull away.

For the first lineman inside the hole, his principle rule is post (Block); if no man on post, down block first man away from hole. The inside-out blocker blocks the first man to show from the hole to the outside.

Rule blocking for a trap at the 3 hole (using the numbering system presented earlier). Rule blocking for a power play at the 2 hole would be similar except extended out one man. The center's rule becomes the right guard's rule, the right guard's rule becomes the right tackle's rule, etc., as in the right.

TECHNIQUE SYSTEM

The Technique blocking system is really a combination of the count and rule blocking systems. The count system tells you whom to block. This system adds an additional element. It tells you how to block. The 224 Dive outlined under the count system would look like this. The technique listed first is the primary assignment. If this is impossible due to the position or shift of the defense, the next assignment is executed.

TE: drive, reach

ST: drive, angle

SG: drive, angle

C: drive, angle

QG: drive, reach

QT: drive, crossfield

A 228 Pitch Sweep would look like this:

TE: drive, angle

ST: drive, angle

SG: pull, lead, block colour

C: reach, drive

QG: pull, lead,, seal

QT: reach crossfield

With this system it is essential that the offensive coaches check and doublecheck techniques against all possible defensive alignments be sure that they are sound. Backfield assignments should be listed the same way. A lot of time must be spent making sure that all offensive personnel understand all the techniques. Various technique that are basic to any attack were outlined. Some of these should be practised every day. Concentrate on those that are going to be crucial in next ball game.

GAP SYSTEM

One of the most difficult tasks for offensive coaches and players is blocking a defense that runs a variety of stunts and effectively disguises them until the last possible moment. When team do a lot of stunting. Offensive coaches must consider gap blocking. Gap blocking is based on the assumption that stunting defenses try to penetrate gaps all along the line of scrimmage, but especially at the anticipated point of attack.

When a team is stunting with regularity, the offense must plug the gaps with angle and reach blocking techniques.

If the offense is using a trap block or a lead back in front of the ball carrier on a particular play, angle blocking should be used. The defensive man outside the hole is left for the trap blocker or lead back, and the lineman over this man either down or influence blocks. If the lead back is getting the ball, then either wedge or reach blocking must be used. These calls can be made at the line of scrimmage.

PASS PROTECTION

In this system every available lineman and back is assigned a defensive person to block. Assignments are memorized for every defense. This system makes assignments very clear. However, if a team blitzes one of the four defensive men not numbered as a likely pass rusher, he may get through. Any offensive blocker whose man doesn't come must immediately look for one of these rushers. It is also vulnerable to defensive pass rush stunts.

AREA

In this system offensive personnel are assigned an area to defend. The interior linemen and blocking backs create a wall and don't allow penetration. Adjustments must be made when the defense overloads an area.

16

TRAPPING

Lot of emphasis has been laid on first time play to speed up the game in modern days. This is considered the natural evolution of the game. But the requirements for such type of game are the things which are beyond the capacity of even a highly skilled player. Because many times in the game, there are many passes which are made hurriedly or for a wild clearance. The player, who has to receive such type of passes, is not aware of these passes. With the result that he needs to trap the ball before he plays it (further). Sometimes the possibility of intelligent move is seized if the ball is played first time, as tactical circumstances often call for holding the ball for a moment. No doubt absolute ball control is not possible nowadays and that is why the players need to learn the techniques of trapping with its variations and also in combination of the techniques of continuing with the ball. In the modern game of football, accuracy and speed must go hand in glove. The principles of last game of tomorrow may be based on the first time passes. This does not lead to the idea of decreased emphasis on the techniques of trapping, but leads to the fact of receiving the ball with top speed. The importance of ball control will remain the same even in the distant future.

METHODS OF RECEIVING THE BALL

The methods of receiving a ball can be classified according to the parts of the body:

a. Foot

b. Stomach

c. Chest

d. Head

The ball can be received with the following parts of the foot:

— Sole

— Inside of the foot

— Outside of the foot

— Full Instep

— Shin

— Thigh

There are three types of passes received by a player:

a. On rolling ball (on the ground)

b. Ball bouncing off the ground

c. Ball in the air

Types of oncoming ball, possibilities of using body parts for reception and the possible direction of continuing the ball after trapping.

For different types of balls coming to a player, depending on the situation, different techniques are applied. As it has been discussed earlier, continuation of the ball after reception is as important as the reception of the ball itself. For example, the ball is continued in any direction to have a safe angle for passes, or to shoot at goal, or even to dribble. Therefore, a schemic representation of ball reception and its continuation has been presented here.

TRAPPING THE BALL WITH THE SOLE OF THE FOOT

Many coaches avoid the use of the sole for trapping the ball. Because they say it is immobile enough. But under certain conditions it is very effective, particularly when there is no hurry, and if there is enough space and none of the opponent is around the player. The other advantage is that the player is able to trap the ball in front of him, that is away from the opponent and an immediate tackle is automatically avoided.

The sole of the foot is used when the ball reaches the player on the ground and also when the ball is received through the air.

The player faces the direction of the approaching ball. That is in line with the ball, while adjusting the timing, eyes must be focused on the ball. The leg on which the body rests is bent slightly at the knee joint. Arms are held near the body for balance. The other leg is raised from the hip and is bent at the knee. While receiving the on-rolling ball on the ground, the foot is raised about six inches above the ground and a wedge is formed with the ground by raising the toe slightly higher than the heel. The heel should not be raised too high because the ball will slide forward, particularly when the ground is slippery. While stopping on a flying ball with the sole, the standing position is about one stride length behind the expected landing spot of the ball. Rest of the fundamentals are almost the same as in the case of trapping on the rolling ball. But the angle of trapping foot will depend according to the flight of the ball. When the ball is landing with steep angle that is almost perpendicularly, the sole of the trapping foot is kept parallel to the ground. That means horizontally, but if the arc of the oncoming ball is lower, the sole of the foot will be at an oblique angle with the ground. In both the cases the knee of the trapping leg is bent and relaxed and the upper part of the body is inclining forward.

TRAPPING THE BALL WITH THE INSIDE OF THE FOOT

This is the most ideal method to trap the ball, and effectively ensures full protection of the ball from the opponent. As the ball is trapped underneath the body, the player can easily screen the ball. The technique has an added advantage of controlling the ball which is coming at a high speed. The inside of the foot trap is used in the following cases:

1. Stopping a rolling ball;
2. Stopping low and medium high ball;
3. Stopping the ball which is bouncing off the ground.

TRAPPING A ROLLING OR A LOW HIGH BALL IN THE AIR

In this method, the body position is almost the same as in the case of kicking with the foot. The leg on which the body weight is put is slightly bent at knee joint. The other leg is turned outward from the hip joint. The foot is turned outward, before the contact is made. The playing foot is at right angle to the line of the flight of the ball: joints are relaxed and the upper part of the body leans backward before the contact with the ball is made. At the moment of contact, the leg starts moving backward from the hip. This movement should be coordinated with the speed of the ball, so that the foot can absorb the impact of the ball. When the ball is in mid air, (below knee height), it is safe to stop the ball with inside of the foot. The movement executed is the same as trapping the ball on the ground. The only difference is in the positioning of the foot. The positioning of the foot has to be off the ground, corresponding to the height of the ball. This can be achieved by bending the knee. The leg turns outward and moves backward with the ball.

TRAPPING THE BOUNCING BALL WITH THE INSIDE OF THE FOOT

Positioning of the standing leg remains as in the case of controlling the ball on ground. The playing leg is kept about 20 inches in front of the spot at which the ball is expected to drop or bounce: The playing leg is turned outward from hip, the leg swings back with bent knee, so that this forms an accute angle with the ground. The upper body leans forward. The ball lands into the angle made by the backward swing of the leg with the ground. As soon as the ball is controlled, the leg moves froward with the ball.

TRAPPING THE BALL WITH THE OUTSIDE OF THE FOOT

The advanced method of controlling the ball with the outside of the foot has an advantage of controlling any type of ball at any height and in any direction of play, if the body action is well coordinated. It is an effective method in an attempt to deceive and beat an opponent simultaneously.

A player must move to the position which is comfortable while facing the ball. The supporting foot is kept within the comfortable reach of the point of impact. The counter action of the trapping leg and the trunk can be seen. The playing leg moves across the supporting leg, whereas the trunk is in the take off position. The playing leg may be turned inward or outward depending on the landing of the ball and the playing direction of the take off. The only thing is that, the ankle is to be brought over the ball. There is a sweeping action by the playing leg along with the ball in a circular half volley movement around the right sole while pivoting on the (supporting leg) left leg. Trapping with the outside of the foot has unlimited advantage of its varying use as the ball may be played on the ground or in the air at any height. The necessary timing and touch with the ball cause it to spin at the player's foot. The ball can be brought down even from the shoulder height with a slight variation in the trunk action which must lean back. The ball is continued in the direction of play after controlling.

TRAPPING THE BALL WITH INSTEP

The factor which is in favour of the use of this type of trapping is that the ball can be brought under control directly from the air without allowing it to bounce on the ground. Instep trap is also justified if the player intends to keep the ball as near to his body as possible.

The technique of stopping the ball with instep is that the standing leg points in the direction of approach of the ball and is kept slightly behind the ball dropping down. The greater bending of the knee joint supports the withdrawing movement of the playing leg. The playing leg which is also slightly bent at the knee joint is led towards the onflying ball and the foot is withdrawn shortly before the contract is made. The upper part of the body is stretched during the upward movement of the leg and bent slightly forward during the evading movement. The ball is shortly kicked in front of the standing leg.

TRAPPING WITH SHIN

Shin trap is popularly known as trapping the ball with lower leg. The ball which is coming off the ground is trapped with shin. Standing leg is showing the direction of the ball. The playing leg is bent at the knee joint and held over the ball which is bouncing in front. The upper part of the body is shifted to the side of the standing leg.

TRAPPING THE BALL WITH STOMACH OR ABDOMEN

The player has to face the ball, that is exactly in line with the coming ball and stands on his both legs which are bent at the knee joint. The body weight is equally distributed on both legs. Arms are hanging loosely along side the body. With perfect timing of the bounce of the ball on the ground, one leg is taken back, whereas the other leg straightens simultaneously. The upper part of the body moves forward from hip joint to meet the ball which rolls in front of him. The ball can also be received by the stomach after making a forward hop on one foot. This method is adopted when both the players, the defender and attacker, are trying to play the ball and are confronted with each other.

TRAPPING THE BALL WITH THIGH

Trapping the ball with thigh is particularly useful because of its thick layer of muscle, which usually is enough to provide cushioning effect. The player faces the ball across the path of the ball. The standing leg naturally shows the direction of the ball. The thigh of the trapping leg is usually raised to the level so that it meets the ball at right angle. If the ball is dropping in a perpendicular manner on the ground, the trapping leg is raised slightly higher than the ball received at a low trajectory. Simply, the ball must drop on thigh at a right angle. When the playing leg is raised, the whole body rests on the standing leg. A little bend in the knee of standing leg support the upward and withdrawing action of the trapping. The trunk simultaneously moves forward when the leg is raised up to meet the ball and the trunk is raised again with the trapping leg withdrawing. The arms are flung wide to ensure stability. The ball immediately is controlled as soon as it is on the ground

TRAPPING THE BALL WITH CHEST

This is one of the most popular methods of stopping the ball, since this is a larger and softer surface to make contact with the ball.

Two types of ball are received by the chest. One which is coming horizontally and the other is when the ball is almost dropping perpendicularly. To receive the ball, which is coming at chest height, the method of trapping, which is known as the angling method, may be used. When the ball is about to make contact with chest, the stomach is trucked inward and backward, so that the ball strikes on angled chest, and is directed towards the ground. The legs are kept in a straddle position, so that the body weight is equally divided on the both the legs.

The technique applied for trapping the ball falling perpendicularly on the ground is different. The player is in a position to face the ball and is directly under the dropping ball. The weight is equally divided between two legs. The chest is pushed little upward , whereas the hips sink slightly forward. The chest with small backward inclination should resemble the arc of the ball. The knee and shin are thrusted forward the moment ball contacts the chest, so that the hip still moves ahead. As soon as the ball is played the knees are straightened following the sudden backward movement of the hip. The front foot is brought close to the rear leg. The ball is immediately controlled in front of the body and into the playing direction.

TRAPPING THE BALL WITH HEAD

The players should adopt themselves to trap the ball with the head. Though it is a rare technique, the possibility and the need of execution of this technique cannot be ruled out. The player is first standing in such a position that the weight is equally distributed on both legs. Body is kept straight with arms close to the body for balance. Just before the forehead makes contact with the ball, the knees of both the legs are pushed forward, so that the upper part of the body makes backward inclination, to provide cushioning effect to the ball. Sometimes, a backward step is also taken to have more bend in the front leg. This particular technique helps in lowering the body sown without losing balance and the pace of the ball is safely reduced. Some players prefer to take a jump and trap the ball while descending, but this method is comparatively difficult and needs greater sense of timing.

REQUIREMENT FOR GOOD TRAPPING

The higher the standard of the game, the more variations of the execution of trapping technique can be seen. The methods of the players will vary considerably as each player has his own preference. Skilled players too have the capacity to cope with the unusual situations, which are not fundamentally explained in any of the methods of ball trapping.

However, ther are certain general principles which can be applied to any method of controllling the ball, which are summarised as under:

1. As far possible, try to trap the ball on the ground as the angle of the ground remains the same. The angle of foot which forms a wedge to control the ball should be adjusted accordingly.
2. It is advisable to reduce the speed of the ball by absorbing the impact with trapping part of the body. The withdrawing movement of the surface must match the speed of the ball. The faster the ball comes the quicker should be the withdrawal movement.
3. The whole process is opposed to the principle of kicking. Contrary to kicking movement, the body at the time of trapping should be kept relaxed.
4. Largest part of the foot, thigh or chest ensurebetter perfection in trapping.
5. Ball control needs one hundred per cent concentration; therefore, the eyes should always be on the ball.
6. One touch for trapping must be sufficient to control the ball.
7. While continuing the ball, the first touch with the ball must lead the ball to the new intended direction.
8. The ball should be remain on the ground or should be pulled down to the ground as soon as possible.
9. The ball should be protected from the opponent . The body must be palced between the ball and the opposing palyer.

17

GOALKEEPER

Goalkeepers were not considered the glamorous men of soccer in earlier days. But now with the recent revolution in the development of the games, things have changed and there is a general recognition of importance of a goalkeeper can save as many goals in a season as a forward can score. But still in training, the goalkeeper is most frequently an ignored person. Every player in the team can make mistakes without suffering from undue criticism. Mistakes by the goalkeeper, however, are unforgiveable in the eyes of the spectators. This imbalance is cruel, but understandable, because that error costs the team.

Football is a game where decision is to be taken within a split of a second. The goalkeeper has to make such decision frequently, e.g., should he catch the ball or push it away; should he stay on his line or come out to intercept? In certain situations there are accepted principles to follow that one only one thing is to be done. But most of the times he has to make up his mind on the spur of the moment. That is why there is no hard and fast rule for the goalkeeper, because you never know quite exactly what is going to happen.

The general belief among football thinkers is that the outstanding goalkeepers are born and not made.

The particular skills required by the goalkeeper are not easy to acquire; however, much depends on how good a coach you are. Experiment can be made by giving two rubber balls to two years old boys and you will see one catches the ball consistently, whereas the other just as consistently drops it. Therefore, a coach looking for a goalkeeper, should seek certain natural attributes, such as the ability to handle the ball ,. courage, awareness of the dangerous situations, position sense etc. Most of the goalkeeping skills are a result of how good you are on these aspects. The techniques of a goalkeeper are discussed as follows:

Before the techniques of a goalkeeper are discussed it must be remembered that crosses corners, penalty kick and striker's techniques of scoring things a goalkeeper must cope with if he is going to succeed. A goalkeeper may often make spectacular saves, but the best keepers are the ones who make the difficult saves relatively easy. The best goalkeepers are those who play safe rather than being showy time and again.

MOVEMENTS WITHOUT THE BALL

Basic positioning

A goalkeeper is always expected to make his move within the shortest possible time. The movements are running, bending down, leaping for the ball or making a dive for save. Therefore, he must assume such position from where he is able to make for any of these actions. He should stand with the weight equally balanced on both the feet with the body slightly bending forward. Knees are bent forward with arms close to the body with elbow bent. Some of the goalkeepers prefer to have the hands facing inward rather than downward. But that is an individual choice. From this positioning, the goalkeeper is able to move using small steps to either sides and not with longer strides. Straddling position of the legs ensures balance. Bend at knee is used for better push off. In all the techniques, the goalkeeper must move his body towards the path of the ball.

Positioning

Apart from the occasions, such as, penalty kicks, free kicks when the goalkeeper has assumed basic position during the game, the goalkeeper needs to react to the play and keeps on changing positions according to the position of the ball and other movements of the players. This type of positioning is altogether different from the basic positioning. When moving to either side to change his positioning, the lowering and raising of the centre of gravity to a large extent is to be avoided. Positioning should be taken up through a number of short steps rather than by one long steps. By doing so, he finds it easy to transfer his body weight from one leg to another.

MOVEMENTS WITH THE BALL

Technique of catching the low ball

There are two methods of catching a low ball: one is catching the ball while going down on one knee. This has proved to be very popular and must safer method. This method is applicable when the goalkeeper has to move out to the side to field the ball, the body is kept squarely in front of the ball. Elbows kept close to the body and in front of the legs, palms are held close to each other, finger tips come almost in contact with the ground. The speed of the ball will cause it to roll up. The goalkeeper bends on the front leg, which bears the body weight also. The rear leg and knee are brought close to the ground and almost in touch with the heel of the front foot. So that there is no gap in between, upper part of the trunk leans forward. In the second method, the player dies not kneel down. Instead, the goalkeeper bends down fro hip. Keeping legs straight, the arms reach the ground with palms out and fingers down. As soon as ball rolls up, it is brought to the stomach. There can be variations of even this technique. Legs instead of placing parallel to each other, one leg can be kept slightly behind (half bent) and the arms are kept in between the legs so that there is no gap between the legs.

There are variations and individual choices in dealing with the ball low on the grounds, but in all cases, the hands body are to kept behind the ball and eyes are fixed on it.

Technique of catching medium high and high ball

It is necessary to differentiate between medium high and high ball. Medium high balls is one which is received between knee and chin. But high ball is one which is above the head/chin of the goalkeeper.

The medium high ball is also received at two heights: One is at knee and below waist high and the other is near chest.

To deal with the ball below the waist, the goalkeeper positions himself with straddled feet 8 to 10 inches apart. Body weight is kept on the front leg. Both the knees are kept close to each other with slight bend. The upper part of the body leans forward. Arms are held in front of the body, palm facing upward with elbows bent. The ball touches the palm and rolls up on the forearm and then makes contact with the chest. As soon as the ball comes to chest, the weight is immediately transferred on rear leg to move back to take the pace off the ball.

When the ball is approaching at chest height, it cannot be caught with the same method. For that ball, a slight jump off the ground with either single or double leg is performed. When hands and chest are wrapping the ball, the knees are also brought closer to give added cover. For the high ball above head height, the goalkeeper jumps towards the ball, lifting one knee to give additional lift and also to provide protection against a charge. The hands are extending upwards. Hands from basket shape with the fingers stretched upwards. The ball is brought safely towards the chest.

Punching the ball

The goalkeeper is not always in a position to reach the ball and catch it, particularly if the shots are intentionally swerved or the area is overcrowded by the attackers, of there is a risk of slipping on the wet ground. In such cases, the goalkeeper should not attempt for a catch, he ought to clear the ball.

Punching should be done with two fists rather than one, and the impact surface is formed by clinching the fists which are together when they strike the ball so that the impact comes from a flat and uniform surface. Punching with one hands is also executed particularly when the goalkeeper still as to enlarge his area of operation. The arms are bent with the fists together and the punch is delivered with a short sharp movement stretching the arms to hit the ball in the centre. The ball should be directed towards a narrow angle to avoid immediately attack again, so that the goalkeeper can recover his position.

If possible, and if there is enough space, the approach run should be made in the direction of punch. But the goalkeeper should not be very keen to have the approach run because his hands give him sufficient advantage to reach over the opponent's head.

Before take-off the weight is shifted from rear leg to front leg which is slightly bent at the knee. The body leaves the ground when jumping leg straightens and the other leg is pulled up vigorously, stretching the body towards the ball and extending of the arms which were bent earlier are coordinated in such a way that the goalkeeper meets the ball at the highest possible point. After lending, the goalkeeper against assumes basic position for the next move.

Deflecting the ball

Generally, it is better to catch the ball than to deflect it. But certain situations occur around the gaol-mouth when catching is not advisable. The situation in which it is unable to catch or even punch the ball, the technique of palming or deflecting the ball is used to particularly combat a high lob which is dropping just under the cross-bar and which cannot be caught; so deflections becomes necessary.

Some people confuse the technique of punching and that of deflecting. In punching, the ball is punched to the sides or in front inside the field and the ball remains in play. In some cases, it may cross over the goal-line of movement and pushed out over the cross-bar for corner kick and it is not kept inside the field.

Deflect is a supplementary element in the techniques of goalkeeping. Any part of the arms may be used to deflect the ball. In most cases, fingers, palm or fists is used. The fingers are used when diving turns out to be short and the ball still is to be reached. Palm is used for greater effect. The area near wrist is used very frequently. Diving is additional requirement of this technique, as most of the time the ball is far away near the corner of the far goal-post. So, the goalkeeper has to dive to increase the length.

DIVING FOR THE BALL

The dive can be used save low, medium thigh and high ball. Depending on the height, there can be differences between various elements, which make up the movement. But the technique of the movement as a whole is the same, with little alteration of the coordination of sequence of body part movements.

A goalkeeper may have positioned himself correctly. But he may not be able to reach the ball from standing position or by moving, because it is still beyond the reach. In such situation, diving is necessary in which the body is propelled quickly to intercept the flight of the ball. The body must fly into the air to enable the goalkeeper to reach the ball.

The ball can be shot at the goal at a speed of 75 km/hour and may be from a considerable close distance. Exceptional courage and elasticity are the most important requirements for the technique of diving. The view of the goalkeeper most freequently is disturbed until the last fraction of a second. If the shot is deflected, the goalkeeper has change the directions of his initial move and must react to the new situation. Experience and anticipation are a great asset to him at such times and his reaction and agility gives him additional confidence.

Diving is an individual thing. It starts from the basic positioning which differs from individual to individual. In basic position, some stay lower than the other and preter to keep their feet apart and bring the hands up and close to the body.

No doubt the technique is to be executed from almost the identical position as basic position. The only difference is that the foot should not be kept so wide. There are situations when the ball cannot be reached by a dive from standing position. On such occasions, the goalkeeper takes some steps before diving. The technique of taking these steps against varies. One is sideways stepping and the other is cross stepping . In taking cross steps the foot farthest from the side of diving is lifted across the other foot. While crossing the weight is shifted to the standing leg, and again it is shifted to the crossing leg which is in front now. Take-off is taken from the front foot; by means of bending it at the knee and a strong push from the ground. When diving from a series of steps sideways, the step is taken by the foot nearest to the direction of dive. The other foot immediately follows it . Then the other step is taken with the first foot for take-off. The fist step with the leg towards the direction of dive is taken only to gain distance but the third step with the same leg is taken for the take-off. In the cross step the goalkeeper jumps from the second step. But by stepping sideways the jumps can only be taken from the third step.

The goalkeeper should prepare to land without jarring his body. This is achieved by pulling the leg which is close to the ground under the body with knee bent. Drawing of ball near the body during the flight by bending elbow also helps in reducing the shock of the impact. Landing is made easy by touching the ground first with the leg close to the ground and then the arms. But when landing from diving for high ball, the goalkeeper reduces the impact fall by using their elbow to make the first contact with ground, then the shoulder and trunk.

If there is time enough and there is no opponent near the goalkeeper, he should try to catch the ball. But if there is any doubt about making a catch, then the safety first principle should be adopted. It is wise to deflect the ball away from the goal. The goalkeeper supports the ball from behind with his hand in the same way as when catching overhead ball from the standing position. Both arms reaching in the direction of ball in front of face with elbow bent and slightly loose palm and fingers make contact with the ball. On landing, the ball is brought close to the body with arms and knees protecting it from the attacker. As far as possible, the goalkeeper should try to dive and land in such a way that much wider barrier in front of ball and attacker is formed to block the path of the goal. The upper leg should be slightly lifted to be ready for the unexpected to happen.

ATTACKING TECHNIQUES

In modern times, the goalkeeper is not to defend merely the shots taken by the attackers, but the behaves like an additional defender just behind the actual defenders. By means of changing the position, he keeps on providing necessary cover for defence, and if need be, the ball is passed to him near the panalty area. This actually is not a defensive measure adopted by the team; rather the attention is concentrated on starting a quick attack, because the ball received by the goalkeeper is safe and he is free to make any move with the ball. As soon as the goalkeeper is with the ball, the attack is planned from the very beginning. It is now for the goalkeeper to make sure that he uses the ball advantageously. A poor start will automatically set the opposing team on the attack. The goalkeeper should prefer to make clearance by a long kick to a fast breaking forward or to an unmarked colleague or a pass to a winger who has the possibility to break through. The ball is thrown by hands for quick and accurate attack. If the defender is near the penalty area, underhand throw is used to roll the ball. In case the goalkeeper wants to pass the ball for a longer distance, he applies base ball throw. The goalkeeper also releases the ball by means of foot, that is, applying various techniques of kicking explained earlier.

Some selected exercises which help in improving the physical and technical ability of the goalkeeper:

When one speaks of scoring, it does not necessarily mean a powerful kick into the goal, but the ability to score a goal. It is seen that many young players are good enough in manoeuvring the ball when far from the goalposts, but they show a weakness the moment they get a chance to score a goal. This poses a great problem for the coach in training because scoring is indispensable for winning a match. So, due attention must be paid in developing this ability.

To acquire this art, the following factors should be developed:

i Mastery of the fundamentals of different types of kicks and heading;

ii. Excellent tactical understanding of the game;

iii. Optimum physical fitness for effective use of techniques and for effective carrying out of appropriate tactical actions;

iv. Ability to withstand the psychological demands which accompany the appearance of a scoring chance.

18

FINISHING DRILL

The players are divided into four groups and evenly stationed in the four corners of the half field. The same drill is run alternately on each side of the field. If only a few players are available, then the drill is run on only one side of the field.

One player from midfield area 2 (or 4), steps forward and calls for the ball to be passed from the near corner. This calling is done silently by the sudden movement of the player. He can also point to the direction in which the ball is to be passed. This player then run to the passed ball, controls it, dribbles to the edge of the penalty area, and shoots. Then the dribbler goes to the corner (area 1) and the passer goes to midfield (area 2). Now the drill is run using station 3 and 4. When this drill is running smoothly, variations can be introduced.

Pass variations

The first variations are related to the pass:

1. Begin by passing on the ground to the near side.
2. Then the ball can be passed in the air to the near side. (If the distance is too great for the players, the coach should move the players in area #1 along the touchline closer to midfield.)

3. Finally, the ball can be crossed from corner 1 to the opposite midfield area 4.

Dribbling variations

1. After the player in area 1 passes the ball, he runs up to the touchline and acts as a "wall." Then the dribbler wall passes with him and finishes with the shot on goal.

2. A defender can be stationed in the penalty area. Now the dribbler wall passes, beats the defender with a feint, and shoots on goal.

3. A sweeper can be added behind the marking defender. In this situation, the marking defender must be introduces to give only 50 percent effort, so that the dribbler can reach the sweeper. (After all, this is a drill for attackers, not defenders!)

4. A series of poles can be placed on the field forcing the dribbler to slalom to the goal. (The wall pass is eliminated for this variation.)

5. The regular goal can be replaced by one or two smaller goals to make the finishing shot more difficult. Two corner flags can be used to make the goal shooting area small; corner areas can be marked as the targets.

6. Finally, the goalkeeper can be stationed behind the goal. From this position, at the last moment, he can signal to the dribbler and indicate to which corner of the goal the ball should be shot. Of course, this situation will force the dribbler to look up as he nears the goal. This kind of drill is popular in Holland, and is used near the end of a practice session before a scrimmage.

The variations here are but a few that may be used from the same general *organization*. The actual drills must reflect the needs of a given team as perceived by the coach.

As an example, weak shooting teams will not face defenders in the penalty area. Strong teams will face a sweeper in addition to making defenders.

These decisions are up to the individual coach.

19

RULES AND REGULATIONS

To nudge or kick a pebble or stone in front of us is a common temptation. So, even if there are no records, we can assume that some kind of football was part of man's life, in primitive days. Stories go about gruesome tradition, that in historic times some races used their enemies severed heads as footballs. The Romans are said to have fostered football as a part of their military training. It is generally assumed that Roman soldiers brought the game to Britain.

The game of football is one of the most popular and simple game in the world. Although the modern game of football emerged in England, in its primitive form it had undoubtedly been played for centuries. The game began in England in the 12th century but Edward II banned it in 1324. His successor Edward III in 1349, Richard II in 1389 and Henry IV in 1401, as also the Scottish rulers forbade people from playing football. The monarchs could not stop the interest of people and started taking a lenient view and football became popular, at least in the public schools. Here were no definite rules of the game, each team played with its own.

An attempt was made by Thring and Dewinton to frame a uniform set of rules but Thring could succeed in doing so only after first trying them out for years. The first football rules were framed in 1862 and were revised in 1863. The same year, the Football Association of England was formed and the new rules of this game were framed in 1864.

An international football match for the first time was played between England and Scotland. Considering the growing popularity of the game, delegates from seven nations met on May 21, 1904 to form the Federation International de Football Association FIFA). FIFA organised the World Football Championship for the first time in 1930 at MONTEVIDEO and the Olympic Champion Uraguay lifted the JULES-RIMET TROPHY named after the then President of the FIFA.

Football was introduced in India by the British. Being a simple and inexpensive game, it became popular among the masses. India took part in the Olympic games held in 1948 in England. India played in the semi-final in the 1956 Olympics. India had, in fact, already made her mark as the greatest power in Asia by wining the title at the first Asian Games held in Delhi in 1951.

The field of play

The Field of Play and appurtenances shall be as shown in the following plan:

(1) The field of play shall be rectangular, its length being not more than 130 yards nor less than 100 yards and its breadth not more than 100 yards nor less than 50 yards. (In International Matches the length shall be not more than 120 yards nor less than 110 yards and the breadth not more than 80

yards nor less than 70 yards.) The length shall in all cases exceed the breadth.

(2) The field of play shall be marked with distinctive lines, not more than 5 inches in width, not by a V-shaped rut, in accordance with the plan, the longer boundary lines being called the touch-lines and the shorter the goal-lines. A flag on a post not less than 5 feet high and having a non-pointed top, shall be placed at each corner; a similar flag-post may be placed opposite the halfway-line on each side the field of play, not less than 1 yard outside the touch-line. A halfway-line shall be marked out across the field of play. The centre of the field of play shall be indicated by a suitable mark and a circle with a 10 yards radius shall be marked round it.

(3) At each end of the field of play two lines shall be drawn at right-angles to the goal-line, 6 yards from each goal-post. These shall extend into the field of play for a distance of 6 yards and shall be joined by a line drawn parallel with the goal-line. Each of the spaces enclosed by these lines and the goal-line shall be called a goal-area.

(4) At each end of the field of play two lines shall be drawn at right-angles to the goal-line, 18 yards from each goal-post. These shall extend into the field of play for a distance of 18 yards and shall be joined by a line drawn parallel with the goal-line. Each of the space enclosed by these lines and the goal-lines shall be called a penalty-area. A suitable mark shall be made within each penalty-area, 12 yards from the mid-point of the goal-line, measured along an undrawn line at right angles thereto. These shall be the penalty-kick marks.

From each penalty-kick mark an arc of circle, having a radius of 10 yards, shall be drawn outside the penalty-area.

(5) From each corner-flag post a quarter circle, having a radius of 1 yard, shall be drawn inside the field of play.

(6) The Goals shall be placed on the centre of each goal-line and shall consist of two upright posts, equidistant from the corner-flags and 8 yards apart (inside measurement), joined by a horizontal cross-bar the lower edge of which shall be 8 ft. from the ground. The width and depth of the goal-posts and the width and depth of the cross-bars shall not exceed 5 inches (12 cm). The goal-posts and the cross-bars shall have the same width.

Net may be attached to the posts, cross-bars and ground behind the goals. They should be appropriately supported and be so placed as to allow the goal keeper ample room.

International board decisions

1. In International matches the dimensions of the field of play shall be: maximum 110 meters x 75 metres; minimum 100 metres x 64 metres.
2. National Associations must adhere strictly to these dimensions. Each National Association organising an International Match must advise the visiting Association, before the match, of the place and the dimensions of the field of play.
3. The Board has approved this table of measurements for the Laws of the Game.

		Metres				*Metres*
130	yards ...	120	8	feet	...	2.44
120	yards ...	110	5	feet	...	1.50
110	yards ...	100	28	inches	...	0.71
100	yards ...	90	27	inches	...	0.68
80	yards ...	75	9	inches	...	0.22
70	yards ...	64	5	inches	...	0.12
50	yards ...	45	3/4	inch	...	0.019
18	yards ...	16.50	1/2	inch	...	0.0127
12	yards ...	11	3/8	inch	...	0.010
10	yards ...	9.15	14	ozs.	...	396 grams
8	yards ...	7.32	16	ozs.	...	453 grams
6	yards ...	5.50	8.5	lb./sq.in=600g/cm^2		
1	yard ...	1	15.6	lb./sq.in=1.100 kg/cm^2		

4. The goal-line shall be marked the same width as the depth of the goal-posts and the cross-bar so that the goal-line and the goal-posts will conform to the same interior and exterior edges.
5. The 6 yards (for the outline of the goal-area) and the 18 yards (for the outline of the penalty-area) which have to be measured along the goal-line, must start from the inner sides of the goal-posts.
6. The space with the inside areas of the field of play includes the width of the lines marking these areas.
7. All Associations shall provide standard equipment, particularly in International Matches, when the Laws of the Game must be complied with in every respect and especially with regard to the size of the ball and other equipment which must conform to the regulations. All cases of failure to provide standard equipment must be reported to F.I.F.A.

8. In a match played under the rules of a competition if the cross-bar becomes displaced or broken play shall be stopped and the match abandoned unless the cross-bar has been repaired and replaced in position or a new one provided without such being a danger to the players. A rope is not considered a satisfactory substitute for a cross-bar.

   In a friendly match, by mutual consent, play may be resumed without the cross-bar provided it has been removed and no longer constitutes a danger to the players. In these circumstances, a rope may be used as a substitute for a cross-bar. If a rope is not used and the ball crosses the goal-line at a point which in the opinion of the Referee is below where the cross-bar should have been he shall award a goal.

   The game shall be restarted by the Referee dropping the ball at the place where it was when play was stopped, unless it was within the goal area at that time, in which case it shall be dropped on that part of the goal area line which runs parallel to the goal-line, at the point nearest to where the ball was when play was stopped.

9. National Associations may specify such maximum and minimum dimensions for the cross-bars and goal-posts, with the limits laid down in law 1 as they consider appropriate.

10. Goal-posts and cross-bars must be made of wood, metal or other approved material as decided from time to time by the International F.A. Board. They may be square, rectangular, round, half round, or elliptical in shape. Goalposts and cross-bars made

of other materials and in other shapes are not permitted.

11. 'Curtain-raisers' to International matches should only be played following agreement on the day of the match, and taking into account the condition of the field of play, between representatives of the two Associations and the referee.

12. National Associations, particularly in International matches, should restrict the number of photographers around the field of play.

    — have a line ('photographers' line') marked behind the goal-lines at least two metres from the corner-flag going through a point situated at least 3.5 metres behind the intersection of the goal-line with the line marking the goal area to a point situated at least six metres behind the goal-posts.

    — prohibit photographers from passing over these lines.

    — forbid the use of artificial lighting in the form of 'flash-lights'.

The ball

The ball shall be spherical; the outer casing shall be of leather or other approved materials. No material shall be used in its construction which might prove dangerous to the players.

The circumstance of the ball shall not be more than 28 inches and not less than 27 inches. The weight of the ball at the start of the game shall not be more than 16 oz. nor less than 14 oz. The pressure shall be equal to 0.6.1.1 atmosphere at sea level. The ball shall not be changed during the game unless authorised by the Referee.

International board decisions

1. The ball used in any match shall be considered the property of the Association or Club on whose ground the match is played, and at the close of play it must be returned to the referee.
2. The International Board, from time to time, shall decide what constitutes approved materials. Any approved material shall be certified as such by the International Board.
3. The Board has approved these equivalents of the weights specified in the Law:

   14 to 16 ounces = 396 to 453 grammes.
4. If the ball bursts or becomes deflated during the course of a match, the game shall be stopped and restarted by dropping the new ball at the place where the first ball became defective, unless it was within the goal area at that time, in which case it shall be dropped on that part of the goal area line which runs parallel to the goal line, at the point nearest to where the ball was when play was stopped.
5. If this happens during a stoppage of the game the game shall be restarted accordingly.

Number of players

(1) A match shall be played by two teams, each consisting of not more than eleven players, one of whom shall be the goalkeeper.

(2) Substitutes may be used in any match played under the rules of an official competition at FIFA. Confederation or National Association level, subject to the following conditions:

(a) that the authority of the international association(s) or national association(s) concerned, has been obtained,

(b) that, subject to the restriction contained in the following paragraph (c) the rules of a competition shall state how many, if any, substitutes may be used, and

(c) that a team shall not be permitted to use more than two substitutes in any match who must be chosen from not more than five players whose names shall be given to the Referee prior to the commencement of the match.

(3) Substitutes may be used in any other match, provided that two teams concerned reach agreement on a maximum number, not exceeding five, and that the terms of such agreement are intimated to the Referee, before the match. If the Referee is not informed, or if the teams fail to reach agreement, no more than two substitutes shall be permitted. In all cases the substitutes must be chosen from not more than five players whose names shall be given to the Referee prior to the commencement of the match.

(4) Any of the other players may change places with the goalkeeper, provided that the Referee is informed before the change is made, and provided also, that the change is made during a stoppage of the game.

(5) When a goalkeeper or any other player is to be replaced by a substitute, the following conditions shall be observed:

(a) the Referee shall be informed of the proposed substitution, before it is made,

(b) he shall enter the field during a stoppage in the game, and at the half-way line.

(d) A player who has been replaced shall not take any further part in he game.

(e) A substitute shall be subject to the authority an jurisdiction of the Referee whether called upon to play or not.

(f) The substitution is completed when the substitute enters the field of play, from which moment he becomes a players and the player whom he is replacing ceases to be a player.

Punishment

(a) Play shall not be stopped for an infringement of paragraph 4. The players concerned shall be cautioned immediately the ball goes out of play.

(b) If a substitute enters the field of play without the authority of the Referee, play shall be stopped. The substitute shall be cautioned and removed from the field or sent off according to the circumstances. The game shall be restarted by the Referee dropping the ball at the place where it was when play was stopped, unless it was within the goal area at that time, in which case it shall be dropped on that part of the goal area line which runs parallel to the goal line, at the point nearest to where the ball was when play was stopped.

(c) For any other infringement of this law, the player concerned shall be cautioned, and if the game is stopped by the Referee, to administer the caution, it shall be re-started by an indirect free-kick, to be taken by a player of the opposing team, from the place where the ball was, when play was stopped, subject to the over-riding conditions.

International board decisions

1. The minimum number of players in a team is left to the discretion of National Associations.
2. The Board is of the opinion that a match should not be considered valid if there are fewer than seven players in either of the teams.
3. A player who has been ordered off before play begins may only be replaced by one of the named substitutes. The kick-off must not be delayed to allow the substitute to join his team.

A player who has been ordered off after play has started may not be replaced. A named substitute who has been ordered off, either before or after play has started, may not be replaced.

Players' equipment

A player shall not wear anything which is dangerous to another players. Footwear must conform to the following standard:

(a) Bars shall be made of leather or rubber and shall be transverse and flat, not less than half an inch in width and shall extend the total width of the sole and be rounded at the corners.

(b) Studs which are independently mounted on the

sole and are replaceable shall be made of leather, rubber, aluminium, plastic or similar material and shall be solid. With the exception of that part of the stud forming the base, which shall not protrude from the sole more than one-quarter of an inch, studs shall be round in plan and not less than half an inch in diameter. Where studs are tapered, the minimum diameter of any section of the stud must not be less than half an inch. Where metal seating for the screw type is used, this seating must be embedded in the sole of the footwear and any attachment screw shall be part of the stud. Other than the metal seating for the screw type of stud, no metal plates even though covered with leather or rubber shall be worn, neither studs which are threaded to allow them to be screwed on to a base screw that is fixed by nails or otherwise to the soles of footwear, nor studs which, apart from the base, have any form of protruding edge rim, or relief marking, or ornament, should be allowed.

(c) Studs which are moulded as an integral part of the sole and are not replaceable shall be made of rubber, plastic, polyurethane or similar soft materials. Provided that there are no fewer than ten studs on the sole, they shall have a minimum diameter of three-eighths of an inch. Additional supporting material to stabilise studs of soft materials, and ridges which shall not protrude more than 5 mm from the sole and moulded to strengthen it, shall be permitted provided that they are in no way dangerous to other players. In all other respects they shall conform to the general requirements of this law.

(d) Combined bars and studs may be worn, provided the whole conforms to the general requirements of this law. Neither bars nor studs on the soles shall project more than three-quarters of an inch. If nails are used they shall e driven in flush with the surface.

The goalkeeper shall wear colours which distinguish him from the other players and from the Referee.

Punishment

For any infringement of this Law, the player at fault shall be instructed to leave the field of play by the Referee, to adjust his equipment, when the ball next ceases to be in play, in less by then the players has already corrected his equipment. Play shall not be stopped immediately for an infringement of this Law. A player who is instructed to leave the field to adjust his equipment or obtain missing equipment shall not return without first reporting to the Referee, who shall satisfy himself that the player's equipment is in order. The player shall only re-enter the game at a moment when the ball has ceased to be in play.

International board decisions

1. The usual equipment of a player is a jersey or shirt, shorts, stockings and footwear. In a match played under the rules of a competition, players need not wear boots or shoes, but shall wear jersey or shirt, shorts, or track suit or similar trousers, and stockings.
2. The Law does not insist that boots or shoes must be worn. However, in competition matches Referees should not allow one or a few players to play without footwear when all the other players are so equipped.

3. International Matches, International Competitions, International Club Competitions and friendly matches between clubs of different National Associations, the Referee, prior to the start of the match, shall inspect the players' footwear and prevent any player whose footwear does not conform to the requirements of this law from playing until such times as it does comply. The rules of any competition may include a similar provision.

4. If the Referee finds that a player is wearing articles not permitted by the laws and which may constitute a danger to other players, he shall order him to take them off. If he fails to carry out the Referee's instruction, the player shall not take part in the match.

5. A Player who has been prevented from taking part in the game or player who has been sent off the field for infringing Law 4 must report to the Referee during a stoppage of the game and may not enter or re-enter the field of play unless and until the Referee has satisfied himself that the player is no longer infringing Law 4.

A player who has been prevented from taking part in a game or who has been sent off because of an infringement of law 4, and who enters or re-enters the field of play to join or rejoin his team, in breach of the conditions shall be cautioned. If the Referee stops the game to administer the caution, the game shall be restarted by an indirect free-kick by a player of the opposing side, from the place where the ball was when the Referee stopped the game, subject to the over-riding conditions imposed.

Referees

A Referee shall be appointed to officiate in each game. His authority and the exercise of the powers granted to him by the Laws of the Game commence as soon as he enters the field of play.

His power of penalizing shall extend to offences committed when play has been temporarily suspended, or when the ball is out of play. His decision on points of fact connected with the play shall be final, so far as the result of game is concerned.

He shall: enforce the Laws; refrain from penalizing in cases where he is satisfied that, by doing so, he would be giving an advantage to the offending team; keep a record of the game; act as timekeeper and allow the full or agreed time, adding thereto all time lost through accident or other cause; have discretionary power to stop the game for any infringement of the Laws and to suspend or terminate the game whenever, by reason of the elements, interference by spectators, or other cause, he deems-such stoppage necessary. In such a case he shall submit a detailed report to the competent authority within the stipulated time, and in accordance with the provisions set up by the National Association under whose jurisdiction the match was played. Reports will be deemed to be made when received in the ordinary course of post; from the time he enters the field of play, caution and show a Yellow Card to any player guilty of misconduct or ungentlemanly behaviour. In such cases the referee shall send the name of the offender to the competent authority, within the stipulated time, and in accordance with the provisions set by the National Association under whose, jurisdiction the match was played. Reports will be deemed to be made when received in the ordinary course of post; allow no person other than the players and Linesmen to enter the field of play without his permission; stop the game if, in his opinion, a player has been seriously injured; have the player removed as soon as possible from the field of play, and immediately resume the game. If a player is slightly injured, the game shall not be stopped until the ball has ceased to be in play. A player who is able to go to the touch or goal-line for attention of any kind, shall not be treated on the field of play; send off the field of play and show a red card to any player who, in his opinion is guilty of violent conduct serious foul play, the use of foul or abusive language or who persists in misconduct after having received a caution

(i) Signal for recommencement of the game after all stoppages.

(j) Decide that the ball provided for a match meets with the requirements of Law.

International board decisions

1. Referees in International Matches shall wear a blazer or blouse the colour of which is distinctive from the colours worn by the contesting teams.
2. Referees for International Matches will be selected from a neutral country unless the countries concerned agree to appoint their own officials.
3. The Referee must be chosen from the official list of International Referees. This need not apply to Amateur and Youth International matches.
4. The Referee shall report to the appropriate

authority misconduct or any misdemeanour on the part of spectators, officials, players, named substitutes of other persons which take place either on the field of play or in its vicinity at any time prior to, during, or after the match in question so that appropriate action can be taken by the Authority concerned.

5. Linesmen are assistants of the Referee. In no case shall the Referee consider the intervention of a Linesman if he himself has seen the incident and from his position on the field, is better able to judge. With this reserve, and the Lines-man neutral, the Referee can consider the intervention and if the information of the Linesman applies to that phase of the game immediately before the scoring of a goal, the Referee may act thereon and cancel the goal.

6. The Referee, however, can only reverse his first decision so long as the game has not been restarted.

7. If the Referee has decided to apply the advantage clause and to let the game proceed, he cannot revoke his decision if the presumed advantage has not been released, even though he has not, by any gesture, indicated his decision. This does not exempt the offending player from being dealt with by the Referee.

8. The Laws of the Game are intended to provide that games should be played with as little interference as possible, and in this view it is the duty of Referees to penalise only deliberate breaches of the Law. Constant whistling for trifling and doubtful breaches produces bad feeling and loss of temper

on the part of the players and spoils the pleasure of spectators.

9. By para. (d) of Law 5 the Referee is empowered to terminate a match in the event of grave disorder, but he has no power or right to decide, in such event, that either team is disqualified and thereby the loser of the match. He must send a detailed report to the proper authority who alone has power to deal further with this matter.

10. If a player commits two infringements of a different nature at the same time, the Referee shall punish the more serious offence.

11. It is the duty of the Referee to act upon the information of neutral Linesmen with regard to incidents that do not come under the personal notice of the Referee.

12. The Referee shall not allow any person to enter the field until play has stopped, and only then, if he has given him a signal to do so, nor shall he allow coaching from the boundary lines.

Linesmen

Two Linesmen shall be appointed, whose duty shall be to indicate:

(a) when the ball is out of play,

(b) which side entitled to a corner-kick, goal-kick or throw-in,

(c) when a substitution is desired.

They shall also assist the Referee to control the game in accordance with the Laws. In the event of undue interference or improper conduct by a Linesman, the

Referee shall dispense with his services and arrange for a substitute to be appointed. (The matter shall be reported by the Referee to the competent authority.) The Linesmen should be equipped with flags by the Club on whose ground the match is played.

International board decisions

1. Linesmen where neutral shall draw the Referee's attention to any breach of the Laws of the Game of which they become aware if they consider that the Referee may not have sent it, but the Referee shall always be the judge of the decision to be taken.
2. National Associations are advised to appoint official Referees of neutral nationality to act as Linesmen in International Matches.
3. In International Matches, Linesmens' flags shall be of a vivid colour-bright reds and yellows. Such flags are recommended for use in all other matches.
4. A Linesman may be subject to disciplinary action only upon a report of the Referee for unjustified interference or insufficient assistance.

Duration of the game

The duration of the game shall be two equal periods of 45 minutes, unless otherwise mutually agreed upon, subject to the following:

(a) Allowance shall be made in either period for all time lost through substitution, the transport from the field of injured players, time-wasting or other cause, the amount of which shall be a matter for the discretion of the Referee;

(b) Time shall be extended to permit of a penalty-kick

being taken at or after the expiration of the normal period in either half.

At half-time the interval shall not exceed five minutes except by consent of the Referee.

International board decisions

1. If a match has been stopped by the Referee, before the completion of the time specified in the rules, for any reason stated in Law 5 it must be replayed in full unless the rules of the competition concerned provide for the result of the match at the time of such stoppage to stand.
2. Players have a right to an interval at half-time.

The start of the play

At the beginning of the game, choice of ends and the kick-off shall be decided by the toss of a coin. The team winning the toss shall have the option of choice of ends or the kick-off. The Refer, having given a signal, the game shall started by a player taking a place-kick into his opponents' half of the field of play. Every player shall be in his own half of the field and every player of the team opposing that of the kicker shall remain not less than 10 yards from the ball until it is kicked-off; it shall not deemed in play until it has travelled the distance of its own circumstance. The kicker shall not play the ball a second time until it has been touched or played by another player. After a goal has been scored, the game shall be restarted in the like manner by a player of the team losing the goal. After half-time; when restarting after half-time, ends shall be changed and the kick-off shall be taken by a player of the opposite team to that of the player who started the game.

Punishment

For any infringement of this Law, the kick-off shall be retaken, except in the case of the kicker playing the ball again before it has been touched or played by another player; for this offence, an indirect free-kick shall be taken by a player of the opposing team from the place where the infringement occurred, subject to the over-riding conditions imposed.

A goal shall not be scored direct from a kick-off.

After any other temporary suspension. When restarting the game after a temporary suspension of play from any cause not mentioned elsewhere in these Laws, provided that immediately prior to the suspension the ball has not passed over the touch or goal-lines, the Referee shall drop the ball at the place where it was when play was suspended unless it was within the goal area at that time, in which case it shall be dropped on that part of the goal area line which runs parallel to the goal-line, at the point nearest to where the ball was when play was stopped. It shall be deemed in play when it has touched the ground; if, however, it goes over the touch-or goal-lines after it has been dropped by the Referee, but before it is touched by a player, the Referee shall again drop it. A player shall not play the ball until it has touched the ground. If this section of the Law is not complied with the Referee shall again drop the ball.

International board decisions

If, when the Referee drops the ball, a player infringes any of the Laws before the ball has touched the ground, the player concerned shall be caution or sent off the field according the seriousness of the offence, but a free-kick cannot be awarded to the opposing team because the ball was not in play at the time of the offence. The ball shall therefore be again dropped by the Referee. Kicking-off by persons other than the players competing in a match is prohibited.

Ball in and out of play

The ball is out of play: when it has wholly crossed the goal-line or touch-line, whether on the ground or in the air; when the game has been stopped by the Referee.

The ball is in play at all other times from the start of the match to the finish including:

(a) If it rebounds from a goal-post, cross-bar or corner-flag post into the field of play.

(b) If it rebounds off either the Referee or Linesmen when they are in the field of play.

(c) In the event of a supposed infringement of the Laws, until a decision is given.

International board decisions

1. The lines belong to the areas of which they are the boundaries. In consequence, the touch-lines and the goal-lines belong to the field of lay.

Method of scoring

Except as otherwise provided by these Laws, a goal is scored when the whole of the ball has passed over the goal-line, between the goal-posts and under the cross-bar, provided it has not been thrown, carried or intentionally propelled by hand or arm, by a player of the attacking side, except in the case of goalkeeper., who is within his own penalty-area.

The team scoring the greater number of goals during a game shall be the winner; if no goals, or equal number of goals are scored, the game shall be termed a "draw".

International board decisions

1. Law defines the only method according to which a match is won or drawn; no variation whatsoever can be authorised.
2. A goal cannot in any case be allowed if the ball has been prevented by some outside agency from passing over the goal-line. If this happens in the normal outside agency from passing over the goal-line. If this happens in the normal course of play, other than at the taking of a penalty-kick, the game must be stopped and restarted by the Referee dropping the ball at the place where the ball came into contact with the interference, unless it was within the goal area at that time, in which case it shall be dropped on that part of the goal area line which runs parallel to the goal line, at the point nearest to where the ball was when play was stopped.
3. If, when the ball is going into goal, a spectator enters the field before it passes wholly over the goal-line, and tries to prevent a score, a goal shall be allowed if the ball goes into goal, unless the spectator has made contact with the ball or has interfered with play, in which case the Referee shall stop the game and restart it by dropping the ball at the place where the contact or interference occurred, unless it was within the goal area at that time, in which case it shall be dropped on that part

of the goal area line which runs parallel to the goal line, at the point nearest to where the ball was when play was stopped.

Off-side

1. A player is in an off-side position if he is nearer to his opponents' goal-line that the ball, unless:—
   (a) he is in his own half of the field of play, or
   (b) there are at least two of his opponents nearer their own goal-line than he is.
2. A Player shall only be declared off-side and penalised for being in an off-side position, if, at the moment the ball touches, or is played by, one of his team, he is, in the opinion of the Referee
   (a) interfering with play or with an opponent, or
   (b) seeking to gain an advantage by being in that position.
3. A player shall not be declared off-side by the Referee
   (a) merely because of his being in an off-side position, or
   (b) if he receives the ball, direct, from a goal-kick, a corner-kick, a throw-in, or when it has been dropped by the Referee. 4. If a player is declared off-side, the Referee shall award an indirect free-kick, which shall be taken by a player of the opposing team from the place where the infringement occurred, unless the offence is committed by a player in his opponent's goal area, in which case, the free-kick shall be taken from a point anywhere

within that half of the goal area in which the offence occurred.

International board decisions

1. Off-side shall not be judged at the moment the player in question receives the ball, but at the moment when the ball is passed to him by one of his own side. A player who is not in an off-side position when one of his colleagues passes the ball to him or takes a fee-kick, does not therefore become off-side if he goes forward during the flight of the ball.

Fouls and misconduct

A player who intentionally commits any of the following nine offences:

(a) Kicks or attempts to kick an opponent;

(b) Trips an opponent, i.e., throwing or attempting to throw him by the use of the legs or by stooping in front of or behind him;

(c) Jumps at an opponent;

(d) Charges an opponent in a violent or dangerous manner;

(e) Charges an opponent from behind unless the latter be obstructing;

(f) Strikes or attempts to strike an opponent or spits at him;

(g) Holds an opponent;

(h) Pushes an opponent;

(i) Handles the ball, i.e., carries, strikes or propels the ball with his hand or arm.

Shall be penalised by the award of a direct free-kick to be taken by the opposing team from the place where the offence occurred, unless the offence is committed by a player in his opponents' goals area, in which case, the free-kick shall be taken from a point anywhere within that half of the goal area in which the offence occurred. Should a player of the defending side intentionally commit one of the above nine offences within the penalty-area he shall be penalised by a penalty-kick.

A penalty-kick can be awarded irrespective of the position of the ball, if in play, at the time an offence within the penalty-area is committed.

A player committing any of the five following offences:

1. Playing in a manner considered by Referee to be dangerous, e.g., attempting to kick the ball while held by the goalkeeper;
2. Charging fairly, i.e., with the shoulder, when the ball is not within playing distance of the players concerned and they are definitely not trying to play it;
3. When not playing the ball, intentionally obstructing an opponent, i.e., running between the opponent and the ball, or interposing the body so as to form an obstacle to an opponent;
4. Charging the goalkeeper except when he
   (a) is holding the ball;
   (b) is obstructing an opponent;
   (c) has passed outside his goal-area;
5. When playing as a goalkeeper and within his own penalty-area:

(a) from the moment he takes control of the ball with his hands, he takes more than 4 steps in any direction whilst holding, bouncing or throwing the ball in the air and catching it again, without releasing it into play, or, having released it into play before, during or after the 4 steps, he touches it again with his hands, before it has been touched or played by another player of the same team outside of the penalty area, or by a player of the opposing team either inside or outside of the penalty area.

(b) indulges in tactics which, in the opinion of the Referee, are designed merely to hold up the game and thus waste time and so give an unfair advantage to his shall be penalised by the award of an indirect free-kick to be taken by the opposing team from the place where the infringement occurred, subject to the over-riding conditions imposed.

A player shall be cautioned if:

(j) he enters or re-enters the field of play to joint or re-join his team after the game has commenced, or leaves the field of play during the progress of the game (except through accident) without, in either case, first having received a signal from the Referee showing him that he may do so. If the Referee stops the game to administer the caution the game shall be restarted by an indirect re-kick taken by a player of the opposing team from the place where the ball was when the Referee stopped the game subject to the over-riding conditions imposed.

If, however, the offending player has committed a more serious offence he hall be penalised according to that section of the law he infringed.

(k) he persistently infringes the Laws of the Game;

(l) he shows by word or action, dissent from any decision given by the Referee;

(m)he is guilty of ungentlemanly conduct.

For any of these last three offences, in addition to the caution, an indirect free-kick shall also be awarded to the opposing team from the place where the offence occurred, subject to the over-riding conditions imposed in Law, unless a more serious infringement of the Laws of the Game was committed.

On any occasion when a player deliberately kicks the ball to his own goal-keeper, the goalkeeper is not permitted to touch it with his hands, if, however, the goal-keeper does touch the ball with his hands, he shall be penalised by the award of an indirect free kick to be taken by the opposing team from the place where the infringement it occurred, subject to the overriding conditions of Law.

A player shall be sent off the field of play, if in the opinion of the Referee, he:

(n) is guilty of violent conduct or serious foul play;

(o) uses foul or abusive`language;

(p) persist in misconduct after having received a caution.

If play be stopped by reason of a player being ordered from the field for an offence without a separate breach of the Law having been committed, the game shall be resumed by an indirect free-kick awarded to the opposing team from the place where the infringement occurred, subject to the over-riding conditions.

A player shall be cautioned if:

(j) he enters or re-enters the field of play to joint or re-join his team after the game has commenced, or leaves the field of play during the progress of the game without, in either case, first having received a signal from the Referee showing him that he may do so. If the Referee stops the game to administer the caution the game shall be restarted by an indirect freekick taken by a player of the opposing team from the place where the ball was when the Referee stopped the game subject to the over-riding conditions imposed in Law.

If, however, the offending player has committed a more serious offence he shall be penalised according to that section of the law he infringed.

(k) he persistently infringes the Laws of the Game;

(i) he shows by word or action, dissent from any decision given by the Referee;

(m)he is guilty of ungentlemanly conduct.

For any of these last three offences, in addition to the caution, an indirect free-kick shall also be awarded to the opposing team from the place where the offence occurred, subject to the over-riding conditions imposed in Law, unless a more serious infringement of the Laws of the Game was committed.

On any occasion when a player deliberately kicks the ball to his own goal-keeper, the goalkeeper is not permitted to touch it with his hands, if, however, the goal-keeper does touch the ball with his hands, he shall be penalised by the award of an indirect free kick to be taken by the opposing team from the place where the infringement it occurred, subject to the overriding conditions of Law.

A player shall be sent off the field of play, if in the opinion of the Referee, he:

(n) is guilty of violent conduct or serious foul play;

(o) uses foul or abusive language;

(p) persists in misconduct after having received a caution.

If play be stopped by reason of a player being ordered from the field for an offence without a separate breach of the Law having been committed, the game shall be resumed by an indirect free-kick awarded to the opposing team from the place where the infringement occurred, subject to the over-riding conditions imposed in Law.

Explanation of FIFA

1. The word "kick" in the foregoing text refers only to circumstances where a player plays the ball with foot or feet.
2. Similarly, a deflection with the foot or feet is permitted in circumstances where it is not intentional.
3. In situations where the ball is deliberately kicked by a teammate away from the goalkeeper, but with the intention that the goalkeeper may collect it, the spirit of the Law is that this would be regarded as an intentional pass to the goalkeeper. Therefore, if,

in such situations, the goal-keeper touches the ball with his hands, an indirect free-kick must be awarded.

International board decisions

1. If the goalkeeper either intentionally strikes an opponent by throwing the ball vigorously at him, or pushes him with the ball while holding it, the Referee shall award a penalty-kick, in the offence took place within the penalty-area.

2. If a player deliberately turns his back to an opponent when he is about to be tackled, he may be charged but not in a dangerous manner.

3. In case of body-contact in the goal-area between an attacking player and the opposing goalkeeper not in possession of the ball, the Referee, as sole judge of intention, shall stop the game if, in his opinion, the action of the attacking player was intentional, and award an indirect free-kick.

4. If a player leans on the shoulders of another player of his own team in order to head the ball, the Referee shall stop the game, caution the player for ungentlemanly conduct and award an indirect free-kick to the opposing side.

5. A player's obligation when joining or rejoining his team after the start of the match to "report to the Referee" must be interpreted as meaning to "draw the attention of the Referee from the touch-line". The signal from the Referee shall be made by a definite gesture which makes the player understand that he may come into the field of play; it is not necessary for the Referee to wait until the game is stopped, but the Referee is the sole judge of the

moment in which he gives his signal of acknowledgement.

6. The letter an spirit of Law do not oblige the Referee to stop a game to administer a caution. He may, if he chooses, apply the advantage. If he does apply the advantage, he shall caution the player when play stops.

7. If a player covers up the ball without touching it in an endeavour not to have it played by an opponent, he obstructs but does not infringe Law because he is already in possession of the ball and covers it for tactical reasons whilst the ball remains within playing distance. In fact, he is actually playing the ball and does not commit an infringement; in this case, the player maybe charged because he is in fact playing the ball.

8. If a player intentionally stretches his arms to obstruct an opponent and steps from one side to the other, moving his arms up and down to delay his opponent, forcing him to change court, but does not make "bodily contact" the Referee shall caution the player for ungentlemanly conduct and award an indirect free-kick.

9. If a player intentionally obstructs the opposing goalkeeper, in an attempt to prevent him from putting the ball into play in accordance with Law, the Referee shall award an indirect free-kick.

10. If after a Referee has awarded a free-kick a player protests violently by using abusive or foul language and is sent off the field, the free-kick should not be taken until the player has left the field.

11. Any player, whether he is within or outside the field of play, whose conduct is ungentlemanly or violent, whether or not it is directed towards an opponent, a colleague, the Referee, a linesman or other person, or who uses foul or abusive language, is guilty of an offence, and shall be dealt with according to the nature of the offence committed.
12. If in the opinion of the Referee a goalkeeper intentionally lies on the ball longer than is necessary, he shall be penalised for ungentlemanly conduct an
    (a) be cautioned, and an indirect free-kick awarded to the opposing team;

    (b) in case of repetition of the offence, be sent off the field.
13. The offence of spitting at officials or other persons, or similar unseemly behaviour, shall be considered as violent conduct within the meaning of section of Law.
14. If, when a Referee is about to caution a player, and before he has done so, the player commits another offence which merits a caution, the player shall be sent off the field of play.

Free-kicks

Free-kicks shall be classified under two heads: "Direct" (from which a goal can be scored direct against the offending side), and "indirect" (from which a goal cannot be scored unless the ball has been played or touched by a player other than the kicker before passing through the goal.

When a player is taking a direct or an indirect

free-kick inside his own penalty area, all of the opposing players shall be at least ten yards from the ball and shall remain outside the penalty-area until the ball has been kicked out of the area. The ball shall be in play immediately it has travelled the distance of its own circumference and is beyond the penalty-area. The goalkeeper shall not receive the ball into his hands, in order that he may thereafter kick it into play. If the ball is not kicked direct into play, beyond the penalty-area, the kick shall be retaken.

When a player is taking a direct or an indirect free-kick outside his own penalty-area, all of the opposing players shall be at least yards from the ball, until it is in play, unless they are standing on their own goal-line, between the goal-posts. The ball shall be in play when it has travelled the distance of its own circumference.

If a player of the opposing side encroaches into the penalty-area, or within ten yards of the ball, as the case may be, before a free-kick is taken, the Referee shall delay the taking of the kick, until the Law is complied with. The ball must be stationary when a free-kick is taken, and the kicker shall not play the ball a second time, until it has been touched or played by another player.

Notwithstanding any other references in these Laws to the point from which a free-kick is to be taken:

1. Any free-kick awarded to the defending team, within its own goal-area, may be taken from any point within the goal-area.
2. Any indirect free-kick awarded to the attacking team within its opponent's goal-area shall be taken

from the part of the goal area line which runs parallel to the goal-line, at the point nearest to where the offence was committed.

Punishment

If the kicker, after taking the free-kick, played the ball a second time before it has been touched or played by another player, an indirect free-kick shall be taken by a player of the opposing team from the spot where the infringement occurred, unless the offence is committed by a player in his opponent's goal-area, in which case, the free-kick shall be taken from any point within the goal-area.

International board decisions

1. In order to distinguish between a direct and an indirect free-kick, the Referee, when he awards an indirect free-kick, shall indicate accordingly by raising an arm above his head. He shall keep his arm in that position until the kick has been taken and retain the signal until the ball has been played or touched by another player or goes out of play.
2. Players who do not retire to the proper distance when a free-kick is taken must be cautioned and on any repetition be ordered off. It is particularly requested of Referees that attempt to delay the taking of a free-kick by encroaching should be treated as serious misconduct.
3. If, when a free-kick is being taken, any of the players dance about or gesticulate in a way calculated to distract their opponents, it shall be deemed ungentlemanly conduct for which the offender(s) shall be cautioned.

Penalty-kick

A penalty-kick shall be taken from the penalty-mark and, when it is being taken, all players with the exception of the player taking the kick, and the opposing goalkeeper, shall be within the field of play but outside the penalty-area, and at least 10 yards from the penalty-mark. The opposing goalkeeper must stand (without moving his feet) on his own goal-line, between the goal-posts, until the ball is kicked. The player taking the kick must kick the ball forward; he shall not play the ball a second time until it has been touched or played by another player. The ball shall be deemed in play directly it is kicked, i.e., when it has travelled the distance of its circumference. A goal may be scored directly from a penalty-kick. When a penalty-kick is being taken during the normal course of play, or when time has been extended at half-time or full-time to allow a penalty-kick to be taken or retaken, a goal shall not be nullified if, before passing between the posts and under the cross-bar, the ball touches either or both of the goal-posts, or the cross-bar, or the goal-keeper, or any combination of these agencies, providing that no other infringement has occurred.

Punishment

For any infringement of Law:

(a) by the defending team, the kick shall be retaken if a goal has not resulted;

(b) by the attacking team, other than by the player taking the kick, if a goal is scored it shall be disallowed and the kick retaken.

(c) by the player taking the penalty-kick, committed after the ball is in play, a player of the opposing team shall take an indirect free-kick from the spot were the infringement occurred, subject to the overriding conditions imposed in Law.

If, in the case of paragraph (c), the offence is committed by the player in his opponents' goal area, the free-kick shall be taken from a point anywhere within that half o the goal area in which the offence occurred.

International board decisions

1. When the Referee has awarded a penalty-kick, he shall not signal for it to be taken until the players have taken up position in accordance with the Law.
2. (a) If, after the kick has been taken, the ball is stopped in its course towards goal, by an outside agent, the kick shall be retaken.

   (b) If, after the kick has been taken, the ball rebounds into play, from the goalkeeper, the cross-bar or a goal-post, and is than stopped in its course by an outside agent, the Referee shall stop play and restart it by dropping the ball at the place where it came into contact with the outside agent, unless it was within the goal area at that time, in which case it shall be dropped on that part of the goal area line which runs parallel to the goal line, at the point nearest to where the ball was when play was stopped.
3. (a) If, after having given the signal for a penalty-kick to be taken, the Referee sees that the goalkeeper is not in his right place on the

goal-line, he shall, nevertheless, allow the kick to proceed. It shall be retaken, of a goal is not scored.

(b) If, after the Referee has given the signal for the penalty-kick to be taken, and before the ball has been kicked, the goalkeeper moves his feet, the Referee shall, nevertheless, allow the kick to proceed. It shall be retaken, of a goal is not scored.

(c) If, after the Referee has given the signal for a penalty-kick to be taken, and before the ball is in play, a player of the defending team encroaches into the penalty-area, or within then years of the penalty-mark, the Referee shall, nevertheless, allow the kick to proceed. It shall be retaken, if a goal is not scored.

The player concerned shall be cautioned.

4. (a) If, when a penalty-kick is being taken, the player taking the kick is guilty of ungentlemanly conduct, the kick, if already taken, shall be retaken, of a goal is scored.

The player concerned shall be cautioned.

(b) If, after the Referee has given the signal for a penalty-kick to be taken, and before the ball is in play, a colleague of the player taking the kick encroaches into the penalty-area or within ten yards of the penalty-mark, the Referee shall, nevertheless, allow the kick to proceed. If a goal is scored, it shall be disallowed, and the kick retaken.

The player concerned shall be cautioned.

(c) If, in the circumstances described in the

foregoing paragraph, the ball rebounds into play from the goalkeeper, the cross-bar or a goal-post, the Referee shall stop the game, caution the player and award an indirect free-kick to the opposing team from the place where the infringement occurred, subject to the over-riding conditions imposed in Law 13.

5. (a) If, after the referee has given the signal for penalty-kick to be taken, and before the ball is in play, the goalkeeper moves from his position on the goal-line, or moves his feet, and a colleague of the kicker encroaches into the penalty-area or within 10 yards of the penalty-maker, the kick, if taken, shall be retaken.

The colleague of the kicker shall be cautioned.

(b) If, after the Referee has given the signal for a penalty-kick to be taken, and before the ball is in play, a player of each team encroaches into the penalty-area, or within 10 yards of the penalty-mark, the kick, if taken, shall be retaken.

The players concerned shall be cautioned.

6. When a match is extended, at half-time or full-time to allow a penalty-kick to be taken or retaken, the extension shall last until the moment that the penalty-kick has been completed, i.e. until the Referee has decided whether or not a goal is scored, and the game shall terminate immediately the Referee has made his decision.

After the player taking the penalty-kick has put the ball into play, no player other than the defending goalkeeper may play or touch the ball before the kick is completed.

7. When a penalty-kick is being taken in extended time:-

   (a) the provisions of all the foregoing paragraphs, except paragraphs 2 (b) and 4 (c) shall apply in the usual way, and

   (b) in the circumstances described in paragraphs 2 (b) and 4 (c) the game shall terminate immediately the ball rebounds from the goalkeeper, the cross-bar or the goal-post.

Thrown-in

When the whole of the ball passes over a touch-line, either on the ground or in the air, it shall be thrown in from the point where it crossed the line, in any direction, by a player of the team opposite to that of the player who last touched it. The thrower at the moment of delivering the ball must face the field of play and part of each foot shall be either on the touch-line or on the ground outside the touch-line. The thrower shall use both hands and shall deliver the ball from behind and over his head. The ball shall be in play immediately it enters the field of play, but the thrower shall not again play the ball until it has been touched or played by another player. A goal shall not be scored direct from throw-in.

Punishment

(a) If the ball is improperly thrown in the throw-in shall be taken by a player of the opposing team.

(b) If the thrower plays the ball a second time before it has bee touched or played by another player, an indirect free-kick shall be taken by a player of the opposing team from the place where infringement occurred, subject to the over-riding conditions imposed in Law.

International board decisions

1. If a player taking a throw-in, plays the ball a second time by handling it within the field of play before it has been touched or played by another player, the Referee shall award a direct free-kick.
2. A player taking a throw-in must face the field of play with some part of his body.
3. If, when a throw-in is being taken, any of the opposing players dance about or gesticulate in a way calculated to distract or impede the thrower, it shall be deemed ungentlemanly conduct, for which the offender(s) shall be cautioned.
4. A throw-in taken from any position other than the point where the ball passed over the touchline shall be considered to have been improperly thrown in.

Goal-kick

When the whole of the ball passes over the goal-line excluding that portion between the goal-posts either in the air or on the ground, having last been played by one of the attacking team, it shall be kicked direct into play beyond the penalty-area from any point within the goal-area by a player of the defending team. A goalkeeper shall not receive the ball into his hands from a goal-kick in order that he may thereafter kick it into play. If the ball is not kicked beyond the penalty-area, i.e., direct into play, the kick shall be retaken. The kicker shall not play the ball a second time until it has touched or been played by another player. A goal shall not be scored direct from such a kick. Players of the team opposing that of the player taking the goal-kick shall remain outside the penalty area until the ball has been kicked out of the penalty-area.

Punishment: If a player taking a goal-kick plays the ball a second time after it has passed beyond the penalty-area, but before it has touched or been played by another player, an indirect free-kick shall be awarded to the opposing team, to be taken from the place where the infringement occurred, subject to the over-riding conditions imposed in Law.

International board decisions

1. When a goal-kick has been taken and the player who has kicked the ball, touched it again before it has left the penalty-area, the kick has not been taken in accordance with the Law and must be retaken.

Corner-kick

When the whole of the ball passes over the goal-line, excluding that portion between the goal-posts, either in the air or on the ground, having last been played by one of the defending team, a member of the attacking team shall take a corner-kick, i.e., the whole of the ball shall be placed within the quarter circle at the nearest corner flag-post, which must not be moved, and it shall be kicked from that position. A goal may be scored direct from such a kick. Players of the team opposing that of the player taking the corner-kick shall not approach within 10 yards of the ball until it is in play, i.e., it has travelled the distance of its own circumference, nor shall the kicker play the ball a second time until it has been touched or played by another player.

Punishment

(a) If the player who takes the kick plays the ball a second time before it has been touched or played by another player, the Referee shall award an indirect free-kick to the opposing team, to be taken from the place where the infringement occurred, subject to the over-riding conditions imposed in Law.

(b) For any other infringement the kick shall be retaken.

International board decision

1. If a player is sent off for a second cautionable offence in a match, the referee is required to show both the yellow and the red card simultaneously.

The Notes to the Laws of the Game have been slightly amended so as to allow veterans' Football to benefit from modifications to the Laws already granted to players under 16 years o age and to women players. The Notes now read as follows:

"Subject to the agreement of the National Association concerned and provided the principles of these Laws are maintained, the Laws may be modified in their application for matches for players under 16 years of age, 'for women's Football and for Veterans' Football.

Any or all of the following modifications are permissible:

(a) Size of the field of play;

(b) Size, weight and material of the ball;

(c) Width between the goal-posts and height of the Cross-bar from the ground;

(d) The duration of the periods of play;

(e) Number of substitutions.

Further modifications are only possible with the consent of the International Football Association Board".

3. The Board once more insisted that referees be much stricter when dealing with time wasting tactics, particularly in the following five situations:

   a. The referee must react strictly if the ball is kicked away or carried away with the hands after a free-kick has been given against a player. The guilty player must be cautioned and shown the Yellow card.

   b. The referee must caution and show the Yellow card to any player(s) encroaching from the defensive wall.

   c. A player who stands in front of the ball when a free-kick has been given against his team, in order to waste time and to allow his team to organise the defensive wall, must be cautioned and shown the Yellow card.

   d. The Board also insisted that referees strictly enforce Law in relation to the number of steps taken by the goal-keepers when they have control of the ball in their hands.

4. The Board took the decision that visible undergarments such as thermopants are authorised.

They must, however, be of the same colour as the shorts of the team of the player wearing them and not extent beyond the top of the knee.

The diagonal system of control

Match Control: The imaginary diagonal used by the Referee is the line A—B. The opposite diagonal used by the Linesmen is adjusted to the position of the Referee; if the Referee is near A, Linesman L2 will be at a point between M and K. When the Referee is at B, Linesman L1 will be between E and F; this gives Two official control of the respective 'danger zones', one at each side of the field. Linesman L1 adopts the Reds as his side; Linesman L2 adopts the Blues; as Red forwards move toward Blue goal, Linesman L1 keeps in line with second last Blue defender so in actual practice he will rarely get into Red's half of the field. Similarly Linesman L2 keeps in line with second last Red defender, an will rarely get into Blue's half.

At corner-kicks or penalty-kicks the Linesman in that half where the corner-kick or penalty-kick occurs positions himself at N an the Referee takes position. The diagonal system fails if Linesman L2 gets between G and H when Referee is at B, or when Linesman L1 is near C or D when the Referee is at A, because there are Two officials at the same place. This should be avoided.

INDEX